# LIVING ON THE TOP LINE

# LIVING ON THE TOP LINE

The Ultimate How-To Sales Guide
for Furniture Retailers in the
New Retail Reality

## JOE CAPILLO

*The Silloway Press*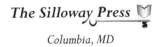

*Columbia, MD*

*This book is dedicated to the thousands of great retail salespeople who touch our customers every day, and to the sales managers and coaches who lead and inspire them.*

# Acknowledgments

There have been many people who have contributed to my work over the years and taught me things that I've used to build my theory of sales and leadership. My first boss in retail furniture, Herbert Jay, is a brilliant man who allowed me to develop ideas in his business. Dr. Phil Jones taught me how to think about statistics and consulting, and the chapter on developing your strategy is due to his mentorship. People I've worked with throughout my career have all contributed to this body of knowledge, and special thanks goes to Toni Lester, who is an outstanding consultant and who encouraged me to write this book.

Special thanks to Peg Silloway of The Silloway Press, my publisher, and her sister Kathleen Silloway, my editor, for making this book happen after three failed attempts with online publishers had me discouraged and doubtful that it would ever be done. They have been a joy to work with.

Finally, to my wife Lynn who worked so that this could happen.

# CONTENTS

# INTRODUCTION

## THE NEW RETAIL REALITY

There has never been a time in my 30-year career in home furnishings retailing and consulting that has offered more opportunity or more danger to independent, family-owned retail furniture companies than that which exists as I write this. The challenges of the 2008/2009 economic downturn offer us all a chance to look at the way we have done things leading up to this point and to consider how we must change our business practices for the future. Retailers of all kinds will find themselves in a war for survival. The battle you'll find yourself in as a furniture retailer will be for customer retention, and your competitors will likely be companies you don't even know.

The world around us has changed forever. Some cultural and technological changes that might have taken hold slowly in the old marketplace have been accelerated dramatically by the recession of 2008-09. While all retailers have suffered during this crisis, home furnishings retailers have experienced dramatic and long-lasting affects because of the central role that housing and home sales-related issues occupy in the overall dynamic of furniture and home furnishings sales.

Here are some aspects of the "New Retail Reality" that I believe have to be addressed by independent furniture retailers to meet the challenges we now face in order to thrive in the future.

## Customer-Centricity: The New Retail Mantra

Being customer-centric means putting your customers squarely at the center of every strategic initiative. It means actually building your company around your customers — not the generic, indistinct, crowd, but those specific, personal, one-at-a-time individuals who shop with you and buy from you. This means offering personalized services to individuals in a framework of one-to-one relationships. It means really listening to your customers, learning about their individual needs, and finding ways to address those needs through new sources, services, and technologies.

Customer-centricity requires that you open your mind to technologies that you previously might have largely ignored, such as interactive website design, e-commerce — actually selling online within your market area — and e-communication initiatives so as to allow you the opportunity to better interact with your customers.

## Personalized Services and Offerings for Customer Retention

The generations of post-baby-boom consumers who are now moving through the marketplace are used to shopping in completely different ways from their parents and grandparents. They shop online until they find both the products and services they want. It is likely they will also will be beneficiaries of the lessons of the 2008-09 economic crisis, and will not do as their predecessors did and buy things just because they can. Saving will be more a part of their economic lives than it was for what I call the "gratification" generation that preceded them. They will still want to be gratified, but will do it for less wherever possible and with more "customization" around their specific needs. They'll want faster fashion, and their sources for fashion ideas will increasingly be found online.[1]

Online furniture purchases will increase dramatically, and local retailers can easily take advantage of this trend for consumers who live in their traditional delivery and service area. Retailers who build a robust website that offers direct purchase and local delivery options can leverage their store/ website marketing power. This will require some investment in web design and management, but it is destined to become a necessity and not an option for all retailers. A smart customer engagement strategy will view a consumer's visit to your store as a continuation or extension of a previous visit to your website, where over 50 percent of shoppers meet you first.[2]

Remember, though, that no matter how some things in your business change, many things will remain the same because shopping in real, bricks-and-mortar stores is "wired in" to consumer behavior patterns and won't be completely supplanted by online, virtual shopping. Yes, virtual shopping will become increasingly significant as a shopping and purchasing mode for some people and for some classes of products. And traditional furniture retailers will have to learn how to do business online in addition to traditional personal interaction selling. After all, Amazon has not put all the bookstores out of business, but it has forced many of them to conduct sales online.

## Strategic Thinking

Every business owner has a business strategy, whether it's a passive strategy (just keep showing up every day and working as you always have) or an active strategy (purposely developed and implemented to provide specified results). Think; which one is likely to consistently produce better results?

Many small business owners believe that strategic thinking is not for them, is something only for the "big guys," and that their competitive advantage lies in better service, being a community member, and/or in a long-term association with many satisfied customers over a long time. All of these things are important, but too often these small independent businesses become so owner-centered that the owner's chain of consciousness is the most significant driving force in the business.

In building a business, this owner-centered mode can work well, but sometimes the Johnny Appleseed syndrome (great start-up but weak follow-through) applies, and businesses fail while everyone waits for the owner to do the right things (or assumes he or she is doing the right things because he's the owner.)

This aversion to strategic thinking and planning is not limited to just small, independent businesses, but it thrives in them for many reasons. In many multi-generational family businesses with which I've consulted, the second and third generations have no applicable business experience outside the family business. When this is coupled with the founder's vice-like grip on everything (to protect the family fortune), there is usually no room for "strategic thinking" as times change. The feeling is: "If it worked for me, it will work for you, because of the timeless principles upon which our business is based."

Indeed, many family businesses see the whole idea of strategic thinking as confusing and outside their comfort zone. Over my career in consulting, my biggest challenges have been in the area of "organizational development," which included the introduction and development of the processes of strategic planning and problem solving. Prior to my clients becoming familiar with these, everything in their businesses was handled ad hoc, as things came up. This led to a lot of crisis management and some very bad decisions, which led to further costly mistakes and more lost opportunities.

## Danger Zones

I believe the worst mistakes that independent home furnishings retailers make are around merchandising, buying, and the universal laws that affect these areas. I say the "worst" mistakes, because inventory mistakes kill so quickly, particularly in a down market. I've heard it said that you can't negotiate with gravity: If you jump off the roof, you will hit the ground. Likewise, you can't negotiate with the universal law of imbalance that states that 80 percent of all results come from 20 percent of all causes — the 80/20 rule known as Pareto's Principle, after the 19th century statistician who developed it. The rule means that a few causes, or stimuli, produce the largest number of outcomes, or results. An example might be that 80 percent of your gross profits are generated by 20 percent of your stock keeping units. Retailers who believe they are not subject to this universal rule are headed for an early demise as they can mistakenly invest too much cash in poor performing inventory.

An almost equally fatal strategic error is the thinking that retail stores are only about the things we offer for sale and the prices we charge. In reality, success in retailing is all about satisfying customer's needs, be they physical and/or psychological, such as feeling good (the universal need); and usually success comes as the result of a combination of both.

This merchandise-centered thinking has pervaded all aspects of the home furnishings business for many decades. As the economy of the country has expanded geometrically in conjunction with the population and improvements in middle class wealth, however, this thinking has had to evolve as well. The age of consumerism that began in the 1950s, and that continues to evolve today, has turned the traditional model for furniture manufacturers and retailers upside down. Some retailers have not been able to change fast enough, and some have not been able to change at all.

The brave new world of home furnishings retailing consists of widely varying formats ranging from big-box national chains where personal selling is not a critical issue, to the World Wide Web, where the "digitals" go first and nearly everyone looks for information, to small, locally focused independent companies where personal one-to-one selling is integral. The differences among these modes of retailing lie primarily in the nature of the goods offered for sale, as well as the varying strategic management imperatives to control the point of contact with the consumer. The strategies, ideas, concepts, and suggestions in this book are for selling situations where control of the point of contact with the consumer is the paramount issue, meaning that one-to-one selling is the source of virtually all your sales revenue.

## The Changing Environment

There are many different strategic formats in play in the retail home furnishings industry, many of which did not exist when my career in the industry began. This proliferation of alternate sources of home furnishings is a result of both the globalization of production and the rise of large, national, multi-category retail chains such as WalMart, Costco, and other national and regional off-price retailers who treat the categories of home furnishings the same way they treat off-the-shelf commodities. As of this writing, WalMart is the second largest[3] seller of furniture in the United States, though it offers only a very limited selection of low-quality, low-priced goods through thousands of retail locations.

National big-box retailers such as Target have created an aura of being smart, design-oriented, low-priced resources for all kinds of home furnishings and other home-related items. The growth of Pottery Barn, Restoration Hardware, and Crate & Barrel as style setters has had a significant impact as well on what manufacturers make and retailers show. In the future, there will be new sources, new companies, and new channels of distribution to compete with as worldwide demand for home furnishings grows in developing markets.

## Creating and Managing Your Customers' Experience

Our world of retailing is changing rapidly as we approach the end of the first decade of the twenty-first century. The "retailization"[4] of our global marketplace — where manufacturers in all categories are becoming retailers in order to be more directly connected with consumers — means that traditional views of customer loyalty are out the window. Retailers will have to take extraordinary measures to keep up and retain customers as the distinctions between production and retail continue to blur.

To deliver exceptional customer experiences, I believe you will have to develop more talented people to manage and enhance your customer relationships. There is a need in our industry to realize the lifetime value of each customer and to become better connected to that person by enhancing the overall customer experience in all aspects of your company, from advertising, through selling, to delivery and service – it all has to be a seamless, high-impact experience that aims to provide a problem-free, life-enhancing experience for all your customers.

There is a thread that weaves throughout this narrative that represents one view and one strategic approach to selling home furnishings, specifically furniture and other related products sold by most furniture retailers. Other selling strategies are effective in producing sales and are in place in some large regional and national retail furniture companies.

I selected this strategic approach because I believe it addresses the quality of the customer experience, and specifically that of a large group of consumers who are not well served by other strategic approaches. This high-service model allows me to take you through a process of strategic planning that is based on good consumer research, is easy to understand, is non-technical, and draws upon intellectual resources from inside and outside your organization.

This model won't be right for every store, but I believe
the principles are right; you have to address your customer's
stated issues around purchasing home furnishings if you
want to grow your business without increasing expenditures
for advertising and promotions. My purpose is to explain a
sequence of thought and actions so that the result — your
unified selling system — accomplishes the goals you set out
to achieve. What is that goal? It is producing much more
sales volume from the same number of shoppers, and even
more revenue per shopper when traffic increases.

Throughout the book, I use the term "customer opportunity" to mean shoppers, and "customers" to mean people
who buy from you.

I've divided this book into three parts:

1. **Developing Your Own Strategic Sales Plan.** This
   reviews some easily available consumer research,
   suggests processes to follow to bring all stake-hold-
   ers together to participate in the creation of the
   sales strategy, and advises on how to put your final
   strategy together.

2. **The Selling System**. This part uses the available
   consumer research to build a selling process that
   is firmly customer based, experiential, and results
   driven, and which is understandable and learnable
   by your salespeople.

3. **The Sales Management System**. Here, you'll see
   how combining the strategic sales plan with the
   overall company objectives and the selling system
   ensures that everyone executes the strategy at all
   times to deliver the highest possible consumer experience for every consumer, every time.

# PART ONE

## *Developing Your Strategic Sales Plan*

# INTRODUCTION TO PART ONE

Throughout my career in retail management and consulting, one dominant issue has caused traditional home furnishings retailers to underperform year after year: The absence of a coherent, overriding, effective business strategy targeting their unique attributes, customers, and strengths. An effective retail sales strategy begins with researching and understanding your customers' true needs and wants; moves through developing a way to address those needs and wants, ensuring that every aspect of the organization is completely organized, financed, staffed, aligned, and controlled to implement the strategy profitably; and ends with its execution by each person in the company.

Home furnishings retailers, specifically furniture retailers, who are the central characters in this book, face unique challenges and costs because of the nature of the products and the supply-chain realities that affect their businesses. Furniture is large, bulky, and heavy, requiring large spaces for storage and handling. In traditional furniture retailing, few customers leave the store with their furniture in hand. Most furniture sold in the United States is delivered by the retailer to the customer's home after the sale is closed — sometimes long after. This requires unique accounting and order tracking systems to account for customer deposits and payments and getting their merchandise ordered, shipped, received, and delivered. Because of this, it also requires extraordinary capital investment in warehousing and delivery equipment to an extent unheard of in other retail models.

The space required to store $1 million of furniture inventory is as much as 100 times larger than that required to store $1 million in HDTVs or computers, and who knows how much larger than that required to store $1 million in diamonds. This is why, while gross profit margins for furniture are higher than for many other retail products, the costs are also far higher, resulting in furniture retailers being among the lowest net profit companies in all industry — averaging less than four percent net profit before taxes over the past several decades.

Because management has to concentrate so much effort on the operations and expense side of the organization in order to control the flow of cash and maintain profitability, there is a resulting reduction in attention to the most important function in any retail organization: sales. In general-merchandise retailing, all that is required is to move the goods to the selling floor and allow consumers to make their decisions. This is not the case in traditional furniture or home furnishings retailing for two important reasons:

1. Virtually all transactions require consumer interaction with a salesperson.
2. The type of selling required for success is highly consultative, skill centered, and relationship based.

Despite this, there remains strong merchandise and operations focus among the leaders of many companies in the home furnishings industry, which has contributed to a generally lackluster performance at the customer level, where revenue originates. The thinking appears to be, "If it looks good enough, and can be bought at the right price, we can sell it." However, there is overwhelming evidence that this is not always the case, and one purpose of this book is to offer home furnishings retailers, managers and salespeople insights into how to develop and execute workable strategies for sales that can be executed successfully at all levels of the sales organization.

# UNDERSTAND WHAT THE LADY WANTS

When thinking about a retail strategy, the very first thing you have to do is to determine who your customers are and what their needs are that your company can fill. Now, everyone who has ever attended a business course has heard that on day one. Yet the furniture industry has been so deeply invested in "stuff" for so long that we have virtually ignored serious consumer research for far too long.

There were many things that I've learned from my years in the business, but one of them in particular stands out as the place to start when talking about strategic thinking. Know your customers. If your customers tell you what they want, what they need, what they like about your company and your products, and what they don't like — listen to them!

Strategic planning begins with some kind of end in mind. If you base your strategy on selling furniture as a commodity, as it was when consumers were so hungry for new home furnishings that they bought everything the limited number of domestic manufacturers could produce, there will be mediocre performance at the end. If, on the other hand, your goal is to provide solutions to the problems real people have decorating their homes and making purchase decisions, you stand a good chance of success.

So, the key question is, what does the lady want?

I refer specifically to "her," because home decorating decisions are made a high percentage of the time by the woman of the house. Our business is a fashion business, and fashion decisions, with some exceptions, are made by the distaff side. I have always believed that there are two, overriding desires that all homemakers have: **creating a beautiful home, and feeling good about it.**

Several research studies performed in recent years by home furnishings companies and publications bear this out. Let's review some of them.

### Furniture Today Magazine Annual Category Shopping Study

Nearly each year since 2000, this major industry publication has performed a study to determine what categories (e.g., bedrooms, dining rooms, living rooms, entertainment, lamps, mattresses, etc.) of home furnishings consumers shopped for over the past 12 months. The study's goal is to determine trends in what items consumers (women) shopped for most. As a side issue, the researchers ask if the purchase was made.

The researchers found that for most of the categories listed, fully as many as 40 percent of respondents who said they shopped, did not make a purchase. To me, this information was far more important to designing selling and marketing strategies than the original purpose regarding categories. Most furniture retailers could use the original data to compare their results with the national results to improve category performance. What they could not do, given the results reported, was understand why 40 percent of shoppers for virtually all categories listed (the exception being mattresses) *did not buy*.

Is it because of the selection being too limited? This simply can't be true on a national basis. Is it because of price?

Price doesn't explain a consistent buying gap across all categories; other research indicates that many consumers shop at between four and six stores on average before making a big-ticket purchase such as furniture, and it's unlikely that all of those stores would be at the same price level.

Further complicating this question is the fact that research shows that more than 50 percent of today's consumers shop online extensively before deciding to visit any stores. If that number is correct, eight out of ten shoppers spend time online seeking both products and retailers. Yet even after that investment in time, when they actually visit stores, four of the ten don't make the purchase.

So what's going on? Is there something wrong in the stores? Or with the products? My answer is "No" to both questions. Three decades spent working on the selling floors of dozens of stores, and consulting with over 100 retailers representing over 1,000 stores and thousands of salespeople, has shown me that there is a huge disconnection between what the consumer really wants, and what we really offer.

This disconnection has nothing to do with the product selection — there is a veritable ocean of choices. It does have to do, however, with our salespeople not understanding what the woman really wants: a beautiful room and home. The disconnection becomes even wider, because our salespeople are more than willing and able to talk about the products, delineating all of the features, advantages, and benefits of each piece offered for sale. What they miss is connecting those products to the consumer's overriding need to create a beautiful home. You cannot help her achieve that goal when you know nothing about her home or the room she's working on today.

Once again, we're all about "stuff," things, while our customer is all about her room and her home. That fundamental disconnection costs us sales.

What does she want from *us*? **She wants us to help her make it turn out that way.**

Anyone who has dealt directly with furniture store customers knows that sometimes, even when everything is right — the price, the look, the quality, and the availability — some customers just can't make the final decision. It's that old "I have to think about it" reason for not buying. Did you ever ask yourself just what it is that she has to think about? The answer is that these decisions are fashion decisions; her choices reflect on her ability to create artistically beautiful, functional rooms that will be on display for everyone who lives in or visits her home.

Most customers don't have the artistic gene that those people who become interior designers have, but they still want to show they can do it themselves. However, they are not willing to gamble and take the risk of making a mistake, because the cost is too great and mistakes last a long time. This explains why close ratios for most stores in our industry are among the lowest of any retail segment — usually in the range of 20 to 25 percent. That means that only 20 to 25 out of 100 shoppers make a purchase today. I've measured the individual performance of thousands of salespeople in my consulting and management careers, have carefully attended to the measurement of customer traffic for stores and individual salespeople, and have found these numbers to be consistent across all types of stores, from big-box to specialty stores. I'll discuss this extensively in Chapter 2 of this book.

If 20 percent is the store average for close ratio, then there are some salespeople who perform above that level and some below that level. The *Furniture Today* research clearly shows that 40 of every 100 furniture shoppers don't make the purchase as the result of their early shopping experiences. I believe the main reason for this is that customers cannot come to grips with the potential design issues around creating a beautiful room and home that could result from making just one wrong purchase.

Strategic planning and development requires that all of the key factors, such as the difficulty people have making design decisions and the disconnection between what sales-people talk about and what customers want as results, be included in the planning process. But there's the problem: A lot of furniture and home furnishings are sold without any consideration of these issues, and this, more than any other single factor, accounts for the low close ratio of around 20% in the retail home furnishings industry. Because "the way it's always been done" works enough times to keep us doing it, however, we keep doing it that way, and this keeps our close ratios among the lowest in all retailing.

## Lexington Home Brands™ Consumer Research on Buying Processes for Home Furnishings

A few years ago I was introduced to some enlightening re-search sponsored by Lexington Home Brands, a manufac-turing leader in the furniture industry. The study focused on developing a better understanding of how women make a decision regarding home furnishings.

### Phase One — Dreaming

This is where a woman will read design or shelter maga-zines, go online to seek out ideas and sources, and maybe visit some stores that she feels may offer ideas to help her visualize her own results. There was, to my knowledge, no determined time limit on this phase, but my personal experi-ence garnered from asking hundreds of furniture shoppers the simple question, "How long have you been shopping for this?" indicates that the dreaming phase can last a long, long time. Women in this phase of a project will tell retail sales-people things like "I'm just looking for ideas," which is almost universally considered to be an evasive move to avoid contact with the salesperson. Actually, it's just an accurate descrip-tion of her reason for visiting the store.

Because most sales training teaches salespeople how to "get around" this evasion by using techniques that are specifically designed to "really find out" what the woman is shopping for, customers are turned off and true communication breaks down. Often, shoppers will immediately take the store off their shopping list because of misguided selling techniques.

## Phase Two — Exploring

In this phase, the consumer has likely gathered a lot of information from the Internet and determined which stores she wants to visit. She is still not ready to make a decision, and again is usually greeted by a salesperson who knows nothing about this multi-step mental process and is just trying to make a sale today. "Are you looking for anything in particular today?" is the favored question by salespeople, aiming at getting right to the point so they can begin showing the "stuff" to these potential customers

Of course, this woman in the exploring phase (perhaps still mixed up with the dreaming phase) isn't looking for any "particular" thing. Ideas, looks, fashion, color, style, and a dozen other things — that's what she's seeking from this visit. There are no "particulars." She's not interested in hearing about our "stuff." This is another point of disconnection between our stores and our customers that we need to address in a strategic way.

## Phase Three — Planning

This is where smart, customer-centered salespeople can truly connect to customers and make customers for life. Helping customers plan for the outcomes they want for their rooms and homes is a lucrative path for salespeople to follow. To be involved in the planning phase you have to either meet the customer for the first time when she's in this phase, or have dealt with her in such a way in the earlier stages of dreaming and exploring that she returns to you for help. We will get into details about room planning in Part Two, but suffice to say that it is the core issue in successful long-term, high-service home furnishings sales. Helping the customer plan the room, and then buy to that plan is the way to bring customers to their desired outcomes, and will keep you connected during the next stage.

## Phase Four — Selection

If the salesperson has done the job well, the two phases of planning and selection end up as one. Here, too, customers need help finding their way through the thousands of options available to them from all the various retail and online outlets that offer home furnishings. They want to deal in a place they trust with a person they trust, and feel assured that they receive the value they deserve for their money as well as the beautiful room they want. The room is the focus in the customer's mind for the final phase of the process.

## Phase Five — Enjoyment

This is the purpose of the entire process. This is when customer satisfaction really happens. For many women, this process is full of all kinds of risk. From the prime fear of making a mistake in design and looking foolish to everyone who sees it, to spending too much for the wrong quality merchandise, they need help and guidance through it all. When you remain connected through this phase, you have built a long-term customer. Ask yourself how many of your salespeople contact every customer immediately after his or her  furniture is delivered. I'll bet that answer is not many. This is the most important contact a salesperson can make, and few do it.

## HGTV and the National Home Furnishings Association Research[5]

This combined effort between a powerful media company and the leading member-supported organization in the home furnishings industry began in 2008 and offered industry members unique opportunities to understand their customers. Early on in the subsequently failed partnership, HGTV published some pointedly important consumer research. Here are just a few of the findings relative to our subject of developing retail strategies.

» 42 percent of respondents (12,000 women were polled) said there are too many options.

» 41 percent said they had too much uncertainty regarding design preferences.

» 29 percent said they would use a source that provided clear, understandable information prior to making a purchase, and that it would make them feel more confident about their purchase.

The research studies that I've cited here clearly support my contention that home furnishings retailers are, in many ways, out of touch with what their customers really need. The repeated occurrence of the 40 percent number throughout these diverse consumer studies suggests that these are the same people — those who shop but don't buy, and those who have trouble with the design side of things. This has been my experience for decades. When you offer customers the one thing they need — help dealing with their room design issues — in addition to a great selection and fair prices, you sell more and make more customers for life.

## Sage Advice

Many years ago, the late Nathan Ancel, the founder of Ethan Allen Home Furnishings, told a group of industry luminaries what he thought should be the mission of our entire industry. Since that day, this has been my mantra and the guiding principle of every selling and management system I've created. Here's what Nat said:

*"Our industry mission should be to help our customers understand how to use our products to enhance their quality of life – not just how to buy them."*

How cool is that? Nat knew then where he wanted his company to go, and he and his successors have brought it there.

## Two Broad Modes of Shopping We Deal With[6]

Some of the most interesting thinking around how customers think, including you and me, has been done by Roy Williams who identifies two shopping modes that we all exhibit depending on the types of products we're shopping for and that motivates shoppers to buy or not to buy. They are the **transactional** mode, and **relational** mode. I find this thinking to be a tremendous help in developing selling strategies and training. Anyone who has worked on a retail sales floor will recognize these characteristics.

Remember that none of us are all one way or the other — I see my own shopping characteristics in both descriptions — but it is entirely possible that some people, on a curve of normal distribution, tend more to one mode than the other.

### Transactional Mode
» Focus only on today's transaction and give little thought to future purchases.
» Fear only paying too much. Price is the primary determinant of value.
» Enjoy the process of negotiating and comparing and will shop at many stores before deciding where to buy.
» Do their own research and don't need to consult an "expert."

» Don't consider their time spent shopping to be part of the purchase price.

» Are anxious to share the good deal they've found, making them excellent sources of word-of-mouth advertising.

» These shoppers won't be swayed by offers of more service or more help with design, etc. It's all about the deal.

### Relational Mode

» Consider today's transaction as one of a long series of many future purchases. The relationship has priority over the product.

» Fear only making a poor choice. Confidence is the primary motivator of a purchase.

» Don't enjoy the process of shopping and negotiating.

» Are looking principally for an expert to trust – and will respond to offers of more help and more service.

» Consider their time to be part of the purchase price.

» Feel confident they have found the right place to buy. The relational shopper is very likely to become a repeat customer.

We have all dealt with all of these characteristics many times over in our careers in sales, and the confusing thing about this breakdown for salespeople is that people are not always relational or transactional; people move from one mindset to the other depending on the nature of the product they're purchasing and on personal influences too numerous to list.

## Conclusions — Right and Wrong

Transactional shoppers shop all over the place, so retailers encounter them far more often than they do relational types.

This leads retailers to the conclusion that price is more important to their customers, when in fact it's only so for dominant transactional types. Transactional shoppers don't display much "customer loyalty" to specific stores — they always shop around.

Transactional shoppers lead to a lot of failure for salespeople. Here's an example of why:

Six shoppers are shopping for a sofa. Three of these are transactional shoppers and three are relational. The transactional shoppers each go to five different furniture stores, ask lots of questions, and try to negotiate the price. Then each one of the three buys a sofa at one store. That's fifteen store visits, twelve failed sales interactions, and three purchases.

The three relational shoppers go to their favorite furniture store, one they trust and have had a good experience with previously, make the purchase, and go home. Three store visits, three sales, no failed interactions.

## Five Furniture-Specific Customer Groups

While the Transactional/Relational breakdown is useful in understanding how people in different modes react to salespeople, I use the following breakdown of customers when making presentations on this thought process regarding our industry-wide disconnection from our customers that I believe is the crux of all the information in this book. I maintain that there are five broad groups of customers, and that understanding and addressing these people's needs is the way to grow your business fastest. This is my own personal take on this based on dealing with thousands of consumers.

### Group 1 — Easy-to-Sells

Approximately 20 percent of the total number of shoppers fall into this group. I'm quite sure of that for one reason: we sell to them. Their number matches our overall industry average close ratio. These people share the following needs:

» They have a need for something you sell. Some room in their home has a lack of something functional, beautiful, or comfortable; or there is something there now that is does not make the customer feel good about the room or the home. There may or may not be other things to be purchased or replaced, but these customers don't feel doubtful about this issue and feel they can deal with any ramifications of this purchase later — the "stuff" is perfect for their home.

» They need a good selection at price points they are comfortable with. You have that.

» They need a promotion or sale to motivate them to visit your store, and you have done that.

» The need a pleasant, knowledgeable salesperson who can help them through the many options you offer and explain quality levels, features, advantages, and benefits to them, and who can close the sale. You have these kinds of people.

» They need the product to be available in a reasonable amount of time that works with their desire to have the room and home they want.

» They've shopped around and your store, your people, and your products appeal to them the most. These are some of the 40 percent of consumers discussed earlier, who did not purchase as the result of their early shopping.

This group likely includes many relational-dominant shoppers who are satisfied with your store, may have purchased from you before, and provides virtually all sales made in our industry, as shocking as that sounds.

These can also be transactional shoppers visiting your store after shopping around at many other stores, or relational shoppers whom you've sold to before. In either case when you meet the transactional shopper a second time, after they've shopped elsewhere, your probability of making the sale is extremely high. Shoppers returning to you a second time on the same purchasing project are far more likely to buy, and this will be a critical issue in your selling strategy. Relational shoppers who have a long-term purchasing agenda are also critical in your strategic development.

### Group 2 — Harder-to-Sells

There are about 30 percent of shoppers in this group, and they share the following:

» They need all the things that the people in Group 1 need, but also more....

» They have doubts about their ability to achieve the beautiful room they want on their own, and feel insecure about design decisions that will have unintended consequences for them

» They need someone they trust to help them understand these consequences and help them see how they can deal with them

» They need to "see" the new furniture in the room and be helped step-by-step through the process.

» Often, they bring samples of other fabrics or colors with them to the store to help you help them, sometimes not.

» ***They need more help making their decision***

» They will buy two to four times more than they asked for today if you provide it

This group contains that one more customer out of ten shoppers that can increase your sales by 50 percent when you provide them with the one thing customers in the first group don't need — more help. The problem is that most furniture stores don't know what "more help" means and, therefore can't or don't wish to provide it. These shoppers are often relational-mode shoppers who trust you and need a relationship that will allow them to open up to you regarding their long-term plan for their room.

Some transactional shoppers, however, are in this group. They don't necessarily need more help; they need a better price or "deal." You have little control over this group unless you can change the deal and follow up to give them your "better" offer, or provide more or better services that they value. If you can do that, you open up the possibility of bringing out the relational side of transactional-dominant shoppers.

This group is even bigger than the Easy-to-Sells and accounts for a large number of those consumers that the above research shows don't make the purchase even in the same year they shopped. Some of these people are stuck in the dreaming or exploring stages of decision-making or can't figure out the planning or selection parts, so they give up and live with what they have until the discomfort of living with it drives them back into the market.

## Group 3 — Really Hard to Sell

This group is smaller than Group 2 but has more potential for very big sales than any of the other groups. They share the following characteristics:

» They need all the things the Easy-to-Sells need, but from a different point of view.
» They need much more help with their room design, and will accept that help from a qualified person that they trust.
» They need to see the room in its final form through drawings, pictures, or demonstration.
» They will not purchase from you if you don't provide this level of service.
» They have large amounts of money to spend to get the room and home they want.
» They will not hire a private interior designer.

» ***They need a house call.***
» They will buy up to 10 times more than your store's average sale if you provide this service.

There are few truly transactional-mode shoppers in this group. These people have a very high need for a lot of help making sure their total outcome is right. They don't want to do this one step at a time, making one purchase after another as they build a beautiful room, because they will never get the room done — and they know it. I believe these are all relational shoppers, and the good news is that when you satisfy them once, they'll come back to you again and again to complete their long-term plans for their homes.

## Group 4 — Shoppers Who Will Buy Elsewhere

About 30 percent of the shoppers you see are destined to buy in another store. You're either too expensive, too inexpensive, too limited in lineup, don't have the styles they're seeking, don't offer the level of help and service they need, or can't connect to them on some level. It has nothing to do with your products, but may have something to do with your people. These shoppers do buy, just not in your store. There are both transactional and relational shoppers in this group.

## Group 5 — Never Will Buy

About 10 percent of your shoppers will never make the purchase they intended and you shouldn't even consider them, because no strategy will cause them to buy.

## Conclusion

The information regarding transactional and relational shopping modes helps us to understand why our salespeople fail more often than they succeed. Transactional shoppers are looking for the best deal first, and they likely want it today. They're not primarily interested in a relationship with a retailer or a salesperson, and may have a long-term plan for their room design, but they will take one step at a time, purchasing one item, judging the effect, then shopping for the next item, and so on.

The more relational shoppers also cause failure when you don't have a way to offer them the "more help" they require to achieve their desired outcome.

The important thing to learn from my breakdown of five groups (which I admit is at best unscientific, but well informed), is that the 30 percent in Group 2 and the 10 percent in Group 3 are, very likely, the same 40 percent of consumers who shopped but didn't buy as reported in the Furniture/Today study for over eight consecutive years. There's a market there for you to tap, and all you have to do is to be creative about how you deal with these people and how to offer the help and services they need.

*If tapping that market adds just one more buyer out of every ten shoppers, you could increase your sales by 50 percent or more, and the best part is you need no new additional shoppers to do it. These people already have shopped in your store; they know your "stuff," and many of them like it. You just didn't recognize their need for more help. Your salespeople sing their same old song, but when it comes time to sing another song, they don't have one ready.*

I'll help you write that song over the course of this book.

# CHAPTER 2

## MEASURE EVERYTHING - DEALING WITH RETAIL FURNITURE METRICS

One evening in my first month in the retail home furnishings business, I had a chance to meet socially with the owner of the business and some other industry executives. One of them said to me, "You know, all we have to really worry about is our customer traffic, our close ratio, and our average sale. If we get those things right, we'll do great."

This was my introduction to the world of sales metrics and the inspiration for my first rule of management in our kind of business — *measure everything.*

Many of my associates have called me "the numbers guy" over my years in this industry. Some people might construe this to mean that I have less respect for the people side of things than for the numbers side. Actually, nothing could be further from the truth. It is because I have a huge amount of respect for the people I've worked with and for, that I believe performance metrics are necessary and critical to both the performers and those who lead them.

Most selling positions in our business are commission-based, or salary-plus-commission, or salary-plus-bonus. In some retail formats inside and outside our industry, compensation for salespeople is pure salary, and there are benefits and negative aspects to all these plans for the people who are subject to them. We'll be looking at the area of sales metrics as it relates to the establishment of your strategic selling plan, because the decisions you make about how to set your strategic direction must take into account all the ways in which your results are influenced by the numbers.

Perhaps the most important thing Yogi Berra, the Hall-of-Fame former catcher for the New York Yankees, ever said was *"If you don't know where you're going, you might end up someplace else."* I add to this that if you don't know where you are, you cannot plot a course to your destination — your goals — so you can't know where you're going.

Sales metrics are those performance measurements we use to gauge our effectiveness in dealing with our customers. They are also the few outcomes you can control through strategic thinking and planning, and through execution and management of your strategic selling plan. This means that your strategic selling plan has to have as one of its goals the improvement of these numbers, one-by-one as well as all together, so you can know when your strategy is successful for all stakeholders: the company, your employees, and your customers.

One of the hardest things for my clients to understand regarding sales metrics as I view them is that they measure the results of personal interactions between customers and salespeople, and not the relationship of one number to another. As an example of the latter, business analysts use many different financial ratios to determine the financial strength of a company. Among them are important indicators of liquidity (the Quick Ratio that is Current Assets minus stock, to Current Liabilities), the Current Ratio, and about a hundred others that investors and analysts use to help companies perform better, to sell them, to buy them, to invest in them, or to liquidate them.

For every company that issues financial statements in our business, the top number on the income statement is sales (revenue). Everything else flows from there. The connections between the income statement and the balance sheet are not obvious to most business operators. To a vast majority of my clients, the income statement is everything, dealing with the simple question "Did I make a profit?" — the feeling being that, if they did make a profit, everything is OK. This is not always the case for reasons that are beyond my scope here, but the point is that after sales, everything is carefully tracked, logged, entered, and reported on the income statement, purely referring to how a company is doing for a specific period, and to specific cost-of-goods and expense factors. It does not speak to the overall financial health of the company, which shows on the balance sheet.

Of course, long-term operational losses on the income statement will soon affect the overall health of the company, so the income statement, when reviewed monthly for the previous month is like a short-term health check so action can be taken to do one of three things: improve sales, improve margins, or cut expenses.

The most important performance metric (measurement) for furniture retailers for controlling the largest money-draining investment, inventory, is GMROI, or gross margin return on inventory (sometimes called GMROII, the last "I" being for Investment). This amounts to gross margin dollars divided by average inventory for the period being studied. GMROI answers the question, "How many gross profit dollars are returned for each dollar invested in inventory?" This number, when compared to the results of other companies in the industry, is a guide to how you're doing in maintaining your inventory balance to needs. The lower the number, the worse off you are, so of course the higher it is, the better you're doing. When there are industry or segment reports such as the NHFA Annual Operating Report to compare to, you can see how you're doing relative to other companies like yours.

I'm going to offer you some ideas on the sales side of things that will allow you to know your overall sales effectiveness, but you'll soon see how these numbers are mostly unknown and unreported in our industry and need to be much better understood be everyone.

## The Selling Equation — The Law of Gravity for Furniture Retailers

As inescapable as gravity, the selling equation is as follows:

> **Sales = Customer Opportunities x Close Ratio x Average Sale**

## The Key Factors

Sales metrics represent the factors in the income statement before the income statement. I deal here with the factors that make up the sales line and how you can effectively improve each one of them to ensure that you maximize sales revenue. As my long-ago associate said, we have to deal with three things to ensure optimum sales performance:

1. The number of customers who shop in your stores (customer opportunities)
2. The number of opportunities you convert to buyers (close ratio)
3. The amount, on average, these customers purchase

Additionally, the number that most clearly defines overall sales effectiveness is Performance Index (Revenue per Customer Opportunity) which divides sales by the number of customers to give a number very much like GM-ROI, but for the sales side of our business. Performance Index is the fourth critical sales metric I'll discuss.

## Range of Performance

The most important and least understood concept in dealing with sales metrics is range of performance. Because all metrics are individual metrics in any business where personal, one-to-one selling is the nature of sales revenue generation, the individual metrics are everything. Depending on the size of your staff, you will find the explanation for your store's performance clearly spelled out in the performance metrics' ranges of performance.

You will also find that there will be fewer people above your average than below it. My experience shows that there is usually a 45/55 percent split of above-average versus below-average performance.

> **Your first, best opportunity for improving sales is to improve the individual performance of your salespeople in the three performance-based metrics regardless of what compensation method you use.**

## Defining the Factors

> **Sales = Customer Opportunities x Close Ratio x Average Sale**

### *Customer Opportunities = Traffic*

Everything begins here. We know this because if no one comes into the store, there are no sales. Traditional bricks-and-mortar stores depend on foot traffic for opportunities, but in one-to-one personal selling scenarios, where interactions with a salesperson are required to close a sale, it's what happens after the customer enters the store that generates sales.

The purpose of advertising is to pique consumers' interest enough to bring them through the door. It's the purpose of strategic selling methods, training, and sales management to make sales. One of those things about our business that many retailers don't understand is this: advertising doesn't sell anything. There is little to no correlation between advertising and sales except for the effect of advertising on consumer traffic. So, when you advertise a big sale and more shoppers show up, sales may go up, while your sales performance metrics may stay the same or even decline.

Everything depends on traffic, but amazingly few retailers actually count their consumer traffic. Retailers provide many reasons for not counting traffic. Among them are:

» There's no way to do it without having someone on duty all the open hours.
» You can't account for people going in and out and in....
» You can't account for couples entering at different times.
» Some traffic is not customer traffic.
» Some consumer traffic is not sales related such .as service, payments on account, etc.
» Some customers have been in before and are simply returning to buy or look more.

When you know that the single most important element in the sales equation is the number of customer opportunities, isn't it critically important to know that number? This is one reason why there is so much underperformance in home furnishings sales, and why so many stores fail in tough times. Retailers often wrongly focus their attention on the things they sell and on their promotional efforts, and not on the way they sell them, so the thinking of higher management is on just getting the right things out there at the right price for consumers to buy. Never mind if there aren't any consumers; somehow, having the right "stuff" will bring them in and make them buy. This is off-the-track thinking.

The problem is that over many decades, this way of thinking and acting has produced nearly all of the sales that have been made in all types of furniture stores, big-box mass marketers, small family-owned independents, large regional chains of middle-priced goods, and specialty stores. When what you're doing works, you tend to keep on doing it because you produce all your revenue in this way. What you miss isn't usually measurable — this is "opportunity revenue" you never see because you are off-track with consumer needs for that 40 percent or more of the consumers who shop in your stores.

> *The biggest opportunity for more sales in typical furniture stores is to improve the number of shoppers who become customers. In other words, it is to improve your close ratio.*

To improve your close ratio, you must first know what it is at the baseline. For this to happen, you must first know how many customer opportunities you have. Too few furniture retailers track this data in the right way, and you must have a strategic understanding about who is and who is not to be considered a legitimate opportunity.

Here are the rules that I follow, after over three decades of counting opportunities:

1. Every consumer who comes into your store for any reason is a customer opportunity.

   There always is an opportunity to serve. Service customers and payment customers are still customers. In fact, they have proven their worth by buying from you and should be treated royally every time they come back.

2. Return customers count as new opportunities. There are two types of return customers:

   a. Those who have purchased in the past and are returning to work on a new project. Developing these kinds of customer relationships where you earn customer loyalty should be the prime purpose of your company. I label these people "personal trade".

b. Those who are returning to your store on the same project. These I call Be-Backs, and you will see that this class of customer is the most important element in improving your close ratio.

These two types of customer opportunity should be considered and counted as new customer opportunities, because each time such a customer comes into the store you have to serve them (again) just as you would a brand new customer opportunity, giving them the commitment of a salesperson and time. There is no difference.

3. Customers who ask for specific products or type of products you do not carry are counted as customer opportunities.
4. Family groups count as one opportunity.
5. Non-customer traffic including manufacturer reps, the mail carrier, delivery people, and other such traffic are not counted as legitimate consumer traffic.

**Sales = Customer Opportunities** x Close Ratio x Average Sale

## Counting Methods

My first commandment for maximizing furniture store performance is this:

**Measure your store's customer traffic.**

I hold that a business that is reliant for its success on personal selling interactions and individual performance by salespeople must measure its customer traffic; if you don't, you really can't know much about your business.

Today there are many high-tech solutions to traffic counting that were not available in the past. A simple trip to the web will turn up a dozen or so good options for use by furniture retailers. What you will not find are many such systems that can do the one thing personal selling retailers must have — individual accounting by individual salesperson. The idea of range-of-performance and the need to track individual performance to be truly successful in improving overall sales narrows the choices for furniture retailers.

Outside sales organizations that employ salespeople to sell one-on-one to their customers use technology to monitor and track individual performance for close rates and average sale or other measures of productivity. The scientific principle is, if you can't measure it you can't improve it, and this applies to our industry as well.

One such system that is widely used in home furnishings is Trax®, a performance monitoring and customer relationship management (CRM) system designed specifically for furniture retailers and other businesses where personal selling is critical to success. It is through many years of using Trax® that I have been able to gather much of the data that support the conclusions I make in this book regarding sales metrics in our industry.

Trax® couples one-directional traffic counting (in) with a photographic image of each customer as they enter the store so there is no question as to the real number of customers your store gets each day, week, month, and year. Salespeople identify their customers in the electronic Up Board by type with simple button clicks, and record only four pieces of information at the time of initial data entry. Trax® keeps track of the salespersons' opportunity rotation system automatically, and assures you cannot serve the next customer opportunity until you account for the last one. In most furniture stores, the nature of our business and the general flow of customer traffic allow sufficient time for this to be done.

During high traffic times such as weekends, holidays, and special sale days, the electronic door counter and the Trax® camera continue to do their jobs, while salespeople can enter their contacts after the fact. You'll learn more about this and other traffic-counting systems later in the book. Suffice it to say that systems exist to help you manage the reality of your business in ways you could not have done in the past.

Trax® also provides each salesperson with a database for all of their customer information as well as action lists and an action calendar, based on their inputs of action dates, that can print for them every day.

Finally, Trax® provides many daily management reports on traffic and individual performance that are impossible to easily get from any other system and are necessary for sales management success.

You must count your traffic in one way or another, whether manually or electronically, to begin the process of performance improvement. Any conclusion you reach that is based on false information will be false to the extent the input is incorrect. I have found that once employees get started with the automated system, they like using it because it increases their sales and reduces their dependency on new door traffic.

### How many opportunities per salesperson is right? A guide to optimum staffing

This is a critical issue in understanding individual and store performance, and I have worked for years to answer this question for clients, readers, and seminar attendees. This is also critically important to determining how many salespeople should be on your staff.

**There is no other factor that is more important to store performance than this, because staffing levels are**

*not determined by the square footage or volume of the store, but only by the number of customers that have to be served. Understaffing of your sales floor is the first, worst mistake you can make and the one mistake that will negate all other efforts to improve performance.*

If I assume that most full-time retail furniture salespeople work between 40 and 45 hours per week, they therefore work between 168 and 188 hours per month. The question we must answer is: How many customer opportunities should a salesperson handle, in accordance with your company's selling system, in that number of hours?

The answer will be different for different kinds of selling systems and strategic models. For example, a fast-track, low-priced, low-service system that is completely product and price driven will allow for more customers per hour than will a high-service, customer-needs-driven system or a design-based system that requires more time per customer.

I've studied performance metrics over the past decade using in what are mostly high-service retail environments, and one number comes up startlingly more often than any other in answer to this question. One hundred thirty (130, plus or minus a few) opportunities per month is the prevalent number. I've been astounded at the consistency with which this number appears when reviewing performance history in situations where there are formal tracking systems in place in order to develop a baseline of performance metrics from which to develop ongoing strategies.

The higher the price/service level of the store, the lower the number will be; it's important to remember that this is an average number for the entire staff, so there will be some people consistently over that number and some below it. However, the most important outcome is this: the most effective salespeople, those who produce the highest revenue per customer, are always close to the 130 figure.

*The 130 number occurs in stores that are adequately staffed and understaffed, indicating that no matter how many customers there are to be served, the most ef- fective people cannot properly handle more than around 130 customers per month. This has been my staffing model for over a decade and has proven to be a good guide to properly staffing a store.*

In the lower price/service scenarios, the most prevalent average number is higher, at 145, and again because this is the average for a group, some people are at a higher level and some lower.

In this chapter, I've discussed the importance of know- ing the first variable in the sales success equation because all of your business starts with customers coming through your door, and you cannot judge your company's effective- ness without this data. Strategic thinking requires many data in order to be valuable and applicable to the real situ- ation of your company. You simply cannot ignore the most important data of all — your customer traffic.

I've shown you one system that has been designed spe- cifically for your type of retailing — home furnishings or fur- niture, where one-on-one, personal selling is the norm — and have shown how this correlates to the second commandment of performance maximization.

Next, we'll look at the next variable in the equation, Close Ratio, and explain why this is your biggest opportunity for generating more sales and profits.

### Defining Close Ratio

> **Sales** = Customer Opportunities **x Close Ratio** x Av- erage Sale

*Close ratio* is the percentage of customers who buy some- thing out of the total number you serve in a specified time; that is, it's the number of sales made, divided by the number of opportunities.

> *The biggest opportunity for more sales in typical furniture stores is to improve the number of shoppers who become customers. In other words, to improve your close ratio.*

In baseball a .200 (20 percent) hitter doesn't play for too many seasons. That's 2 hits for every 10 times at bat, 20 hits for every 100 times at bat. On the other hand, a .300 hitter gets into the Baseball Hall of Fame. That means that one more hit out of ten tries, 10 more in 100 times at bat, is the difference between failure and stardom.

The same goes for furniture retailers. If you are a 20 percent closer and you can find a way to close just 1 more out of every 10 shoppers, 10 out of every 100 opportunities, your sales and your income (if you're on commission) go up by 50 percent! Why? Because three is 50 percent larger than two.

Few business owners or managers I have encountered over the years are aware of their true close ratio. Many believe their close rates are 50 percent or higher, and because of this lack of awareness of their actual numbers they do not understand the opportunity for improvement to be as large as it truly is. If you want to see just how great the opportunity is, read on, please.

Let's look at the results of over two years of careful study of actual performance records in a mid-priced, full-line furniture store with 20 salespeople in a sub-metro market of just under one million in population. The store had average annual total shopper foot traffic of 20,000.

» The close ratio for shoppers on their *first* visit to the store on a specific home furnishings project is 10 percent on average — one customer in ten makes the purchase on their first visit. Eight of the 20 salespeople performed above that number, with the high being 14.3 percent, and 12 performed below that level, with the low being six percent.

> ❧ The close ratio of shoppers on their *second* visit is 75 percent, with the high being over 90 percent and the low being 65 percent.

These figures carried through two years of traffic, and they match almost perfectly my experience with another group of six branded stores in a similar study lasting one year.

> ❧ The overall closing ratio for this store during this two-year study was 20.5 percent.
> ❧ The highest individual close ratio was 32 percent; this person also had the highest number of Be-Back customers (15-20 percent of his monthly opportunities).

I include this data in the definition section to emphasize the strategic nature of performance data. Strategically, based on the above, we have to develop ways to sell more people the first time we meet them, and to get the non-buyers back again, keeping in mind our 40 percent of non-buyers.

Close ratio is a reflection of several things relative to how salespeople **connect** to customers:

> ❧ The ability to greet warmly and actually engage shoppers
> ❧ The level of trust developed by the salesperson
> ❧ The ability to deal with the real issues the customer is facing around the purchasing decision — as in dealing with rooms
> ❧ The ability to earn and develop Be-Back appointments

This begins to explain why so many furniture stores underperform relative to the apparent consumer need that exists for our products and services, relative to the number of consumers who shop in our stores.

## Defining Average Sale

> Sales = Customer Opportunities x Close Ratio x **Average Sale**

First, a caution. Average sale and average *ticket* are not the same thing. In some stores they may be, but you need to be careful about using average ticket numbers from your computer systems, because they are skewed based on the way you enter different categories of sales for system, accounting, or order-processing purposes.

Simply put, a customer purchases $3,000 in furniture from stock, $2,000 of furniture as special order, and $1,000 in accessories that they take with them. Some stores enter three tickets, which would make the average ticket $2,000, while the sale made to this customer by this salesperson was actually $6,000.

> *Average sale is the total amount a customer purchases at one time, added to the total amount purchased by all other customers for the day, divided by the total number of purchases made that day.*

Average sale is calculated by day. Tomorrow's sales to these same customers are separate. I have always done this because of the cumbersome calculations required, even with sophisticated computer operating systems, to combine sales across different days. Additionally, sales made one, two, or any number of days after the original sale might never have been made. Anything can happen to change a customer's mind or affect their decision or ability to buy. ***New decisions means new sales are closed***.

Average sale is a direct reflection of how salespeople **work with** their customers. Over time, as you measure each individual's cumulative average, you will clearly see that another huge opportunity to improve sales lies in closing the performance gap between your top performers in each of the sales metrics. This involves maintaining or improving the top numbers and incrementally improving the bottom numbers, thereby raising your ship as a whole. You need to raise the tide.

Average sale, along with close ratio, are the two performance results metrics that tell you how your people are working with customers and point to specific areas of training that is will help your people improve their performance.

## Return Customers (Be-Backs)

Additionally, there is one metric that I use to know quickly whether there is a specific need that can be addressed systemically to help individual salespeople perform better. One of the first places I look to know how to help a salesperson or a store improve is their number and percentage of Be-Back customers over the short and long term. I know that if a salesperson is recording 15 percent or higher of their total customer opportunities as Be-Backs, their closing ratio will be far higher than if they are below this number because these return customers make purchases 75 percent of the time. I also know that return visits by customers to specific salespeople are earned by the salesperson through dealing properly with the customer on their first visit.

This is important to note because it is through developing return visits by current shoppers that salespeople affect their customer opportunities. They do not improve the **quantity** because of the 130 guideline, but they dramatically improve the **quality** of the opportunities they get.

### Revenue-per-Opportunity (RPU) – Your Overall measure of Sales Effectiveness

Also known as performance index (PI), or effectiveness index, this is the measure of overall effectiveness for salespeople and sales departments. It takes into account the effects of both close ratio and average sale, and it is a critical metric to know when analyzing which people need coaching and training. This is the owner and manager's overall sales-effectiveness measure.

Simply put, this metric is based on sales divided by opportunities (shoppers) and answers the question: **How many dollars can we put in the bank for every customer who comes through our doors?**

You will see a range of performance in this metric, just as you do with close ratio and average sale. The issue for owners, managers, and salespeople is that, because of their efforts to be fair and provide all salespeople with an equal number of opportunities, they receive a very unequal return for their efforts.

You can arrive at the same RPU (PI) in two different ways. You can have a low close ratio and high average sale, or vice versa, and have the same RPU.

130 Opportunities x 25 percent Close Ratio x $1,040 Average Sale = $33,800 Sales.
$33,800 ÷ 130 = $260 per customer opportunity.

130 Opportunities x 15 percent Close Ratio x $1,733.33 Average Sale = $33,800 Sales
This also provides $260 per customer opportunity.

This example demonstrates how this metric is a management measure for understanding what can happen with targeted performance improvement. In this example, one salesperson needs to improve her average sale, while the other has to improve his close ratio.

## Calculating Your Lost Sales Volume

This is one of the most important reasons to keep your metrics up to date and make the required investment in gathering them. For virtually any size store, this metric will help you recognize lost sales volume of 15 percent or more that is due entirely to below-average performance by individual salespeople in close ratio or average sale. Here's how it works:

- ❧ Determine your store averages for close ratio and average sale.
- ❧ Look at each individual's numbers and determine who is under the store's average for each of the two factors — close ratio and average sale.
- ❧ Calculate how much more business would have been written if these people performed at just the average level in each of the factors.
- ❧ Then calculate what your store averages for both factors would have been under this improved scenario.

In this exercise, you are looking at a reasonable expectation, because you're not thinking that everyone should perform at the top of the scale. In fact, those people who are over the average (the best of the worst) in both close ratio and average sale don't have to change anything. You are simply attempting to define what your first level improvement goals should be.

Another simple way to come to this is to multiply your highest RPU value times your total number of opportunities to determine what your total sales opportunity is.

What you now have are goals for performance for both your store and those individuals who are performing below the store's averages. What you need are ways to teach, train and coach individuals to reach these clearly calculated performance levels in two specific areas: close ratio and average sale.

You are at the beginning stage of understanding why you need a selling strategy. If you could calculate any other opportunity in your business with such accuracy, you would do it in a minute. If you could run an ad or buy some product that would guarantee to improve your sales by 15 percent, you'd jump on it. And, the best things of all about this opportunity are these:

» You don't need to spend one more advertising dollar than you're now spending.

» You don't need any more customers than you're now getting — they've already been here, shopped, but didn't buy for reasons other than your products, prices, or promotions. They simply needed more help!

» You simply have to give your salespeople methods, systems, training, and coaching to get a minimum 15 percent increase in revenue.

To do this you have to begin to think differently and throw aside all your preconceived ideas about what our business is really all about. You have to overcome the limiting thinking that the answers to generating more profit somehow lie outside yourself and your influence, or in doing better the things you've already been doing. You have to open your mind to new ideas and new ways of doing things because your customers **have told you what they want**. In addition, you have to believe the one thing I believe is missing from the collective thinking of our industry:

> **Our business is not about furniture, it's about ROOMS!**

This way of thinking about your business is the necessary paradigm shift required to move from being a merchandise-centered company to being a customer-centered company. Some smart companies in our industry know this. When the Seaman family chose a name for their spectacularly successful company, they did not call it Furniture-to-Go. They called it **Rooms-to-Go**.

## Summary

In Chapters 1 and 2, you've learned that strategic thinking and planning require knowledge of your customers and of your business. It needs to use research on customer thinking and behavior and draw on facts regarding how your business really works. This research is available from many sources, including industry publications and organizations, and can be obtained form some sources free, but also is available on a charge basis from sources on line or through industry sources.

The research is fundamental to knowing your customers' unexpressed needs and their issues around purchasing your products and services.

Your own performance history is in your hands but is usually not in a form you can use effectively to manage on a day-to-day basis. For this, you need an information-gathering and reporting system specifically designed for your business that gives you the data I discussed in this chapter.

You have seen how a few important performance metrics can provide a snapshot look at how things are going, and how to use this information to know why things are going that way. And you have seen how to use the metrics for determining where you can go.

Next, in Chapter 3, you'll learn how to use all the research and performance data to develop a written selling strategy and selling system to address each of the needs we see in research and to improve each of the performance metrics to make more sales and profits.

# PUTTING YOUR SELLING STRATEGY TOGETHER

## Step 1 — Use the Research

If you have research, use it. Sounds like simple common sense, but I am aware of few home furnishings retailers who use any of the research that comes their way to change the way they do things. Those who do — usually the large regional or national companies — have a more strategic view of their businesses than smaller, independent companies that are usually far too owner-centric to look at national results and believe that their markets, their customers, and their situation is different. They aren't different. In too many cases, only the results are different, and in challenging times, the companies with a customer-centered strategy that is based on solid consumer research, and that have aligned all aspects of their organizations with the strategic goals, win out.

What the woman wants is clearly spelled out in the research I presented above, and her pathway to achievement of that goal may go through many different distribution channels in today's information-based consumer environment. If you're a bricks-and-mortar retailer, you need to be strategically ready to help her on her journey to beautiful rooms and homes. This means that your selling system, your management systems, your merchandising plan, and sales services including delivery and after-the delivery services must all be focused on creating beautiful rooms and homes, and a high-quality customer experience no matter your level of involvement or the size of your customer's purchase. Every item of furniture or accessories you sell is going to be part of some room, somewhere, and is far more important to your customer than you often think it is.

What we have learned so far from outside research:

» 40 percent, almost half, of furniture shoppers report that they did not make a purchase as the result of their initial shopping experience. Remember, the polling takes place in January of each year and results reported in February. Some of those polled could have shopped in January of the prior year, and some in December. Because polling is random, there is no way to tell how much time passes between store visits or exactly when people shopped over the year.

» In a separate study of over 12,000 people, 41 percent of respondents stated that there are too many options available in home furnishings and furniture.

» 41 percent also stated that they needed help with the design aspects of their decision to purchase.

» There is a progression of thought and action that operates over time in the decision making process around making a change to a room. Understanding where a customer is in the process requires a high level of customer engagement skills, and is important in the overall scheme of selling furniture.

So, when you look at all the research you know that there is a very large opportunity with nearly 40 out of every 100 shoppers in any store, to help them resolve problems around how to use our products in their home — meaning, how to work out the "design" issues.

The key issue is that this 40 percent figure is a rolling number. Every month 40 percent of shoppers will struggle with the vast number of options available as they go from store to store and be unable to make a decision. Forty percent will not be able to mentally deal with the effect that this purchase will have on other furniture they own, or intend to buy. They will be unable to come to terms with color flow issues between rooms and other areas, and they will not be able to visualize the result, a beautiful, complete room, as being easily achievable for them.

The important part of all this for furniture retailers is that there are, at any given time, thousands of consumers who have shopped in your stores but who have not made a purchase. Forty percent is a significant number, but this does not represent a stagnant number of people. The people change as some of the non-buyers make their purchases after additional shopping, perhaps even from one of the stores they shopped in early in the process, but these people are replaced by new shoppers who begin a project, make their store visits, and do not make a purchase.

## Furniture Emergencies? — Not Really

There are few "furniture" emergencies that cause people to buy high-ticket items, particularly in the replacement segment of the market. It's not the same to want a new sofa as it is to need a new refrigerator when yours fails. Most furniture purchases are easily delayed, which means that shopping for it is not an immediate priority for most people. They shop when they have time, or are near a store, or have received some kind of appealing sale offer from a store. In other words, when we hold a promotion, our increased sales revenue comes from attracting more customers to the event than would shop otherwise, not from improved closing ratios.

Price is an important influence on how some transactional customers buy, but it is not the most important influence.

There are all kinds of personal events that force consumers to make a purchase, such as family visits and social events (weddings, graduations, birthdays, etc.), and all of us have encountered this kind of immediacy among our customers. Still, the overwhelming numbers of customers have no outside-influenced deadlines on making furniture or home furnishings purchases. The decision to purchase is internally driven and tied directly to your customer's desire (need) for beautiful, functional, comfortable rooms in which to live.

It is my belief that all furniture and home furnishings purchases are rooted in the universal need to create pleasing, if not beautiful, comfortable, functional home environments for one's family. Additionally, I believe that there is a deeper, underlying need that is at the root of all of our lives — **to feel good**. We all do things, think things, buy things, and want things that make us feel good, because that is the core purpose in human beings. It is this basic need that drives virtually all actions we take, thoughts (both conscious and unconscious) we generate. Making the purchase decision is your customer's effort to feel good. It's not just furniture, it's quality of life.

## START

### Step 2 — Build Your Strategy Development Team

When you build your Strategy Development Team, involve as many people from as many different areas of your business as possible. This will ensure that all the people who have a stake in your business being successful are fully involved from the beginning. Have at least one representative from every department participate in order to accomplish complete alignment of purpose and effort across your company.

Two of the worst mistakes made by small independent businesses, particularly family-owned and -operated businesses, is to be too owner-centered or too sibling-divided, which ends up closing out whole areas of valuable input because of family jealousies and "silo" thinking.

Your organization is organic in nature because it is nothing more than the sum of the work of your employees. Look at all the interdependencies there are as we identify the people who should be involved in your strategic selling plan.

### The Owner or Top Dog

It's amazing how many company initiatives began and failed because the head person was not involved and fully committed to the idea from the start. This is the number one reason why corporate change initiatives fail — no commitment from the top.

### All Department Heads

This may seem obvious, but I've witnessed many examples of silo management around important strategic initiatives that went awry due to little or no buy in by all departments. If anything you do requires some degree of execution by any person or department, they need to be involved from the beginning and throughout the entire process. What you are seeking is alignment in all areas behind the strategic plan of your company. You need to involve everyone who engages with your customers or who affects customer relations.

Here are the back-office departments that should be in on the ground floor of the planning:

- » Advertising, because they will tell your story designed to bring in the right customers with needs you can fulfill. Nothing is worse than to be misaligned at this level.
- » Merchandising and purchasing, because your new strategy may require new and different things to

be presented to your customers, and new and different display, tagging, and point-of-sale material. The story needs to be in full alignment throughout the company.

» Accounting, because customer accounts are handled here. Deposits are tracked, refunds are issued, finance issues handled, and there is direct customer contact with these folks. Maintaining customer accounts is an important part of your relationship with your customers.

» Order Processing, because tracking open orders, special orders, purchase orders, etc., are all things that affect overall customer relations and service. When a new sales initiative is established, there needs to be training of and support from all parts of your company.

» Customer Service, because these people have extensive customer contact and affect your customers' experience with your company. I think of customer service people as extensions of the sales force. They are extremely important to your customers' experiences.

» Delivery and warehousing, because these are often the last people to see your customers. Their ability to positively or negatively affect your customers' experience and future decisions is almost universally underestimated. These are the people who deliver the final satisfaction for the customer.

Commitment and buy-in come from participation in the process.

### Sales Department Representatives

Put some of your salespeople on the development team. Let the team decide who should represent them. This is the best way to avoid any us/them thinking that almost always exists in stores when a new idea or strategy. The sales force comprises the very people most affected by changing strategies.

Let them participate in writing their song.

## Step 3 — Create Your Mission Statement

Nothing forms a foundation for work, communications, organizational purpose, and achievement as well as your statement of mission. It is your way of demonstrating that the character of your company is on the highest possible plane of service. However, if you do not intend to live by this mission, if you drift from day to day managing only the things that happen and responding in ways that "depend" on the circumstances, then don't develop or publish a mission statement.

With this warning in mind, here is what I suggest be in your mission statement:

> ❧ Your statement of purpose as a company. Your purpose is not to "make a profit"; that is the **definition** of every commercial company. Think of what you would say about your company if it were a non-profit organization — why would your organization exist? Making a profit doing what you do is definitive of a business, and is never necessary in a mission statement. Your mission should reflect the outcomes for the people you serve.

> ❧ Include reference to all of the stakeholders involved in your company — both inside and outside your employment rolls. For example, your employees, your customers, and your suppliers need to be part of your mission — they all have a stake.

Here's my suggested universal mission statement for home furnishings retail companies:

*It is our mission to serve our community by helping our customers understand how to use our home furnishings products to enhance the beauty and comfort of their homes and the quality of their lives. We will provide fair value to our customers, and will represent our suppliers with honor and integrity at all times. We will strive to provide a high-quality workplace where our employees can prosper and achieve their quality-of-life goals.*

We are not promising the "best" prices, the "best" quality, or the "best" values, because every company in our business can make those kinds of claims. What's best is often in the mind of the customer and what that person is looking for as an outcome. Price is relative to quality and your customer's ability to buy. There will be many other factors that go into a customer's decision to buy from your store, mostly related to how you deal with them as opposed to only what you carry.

You can live up to this mission statement. Everyone who works in your company can do things every day to live up to it. You can point to this when there are behavioral conflicts by members of your company (as long as you yourself live up to it every day) and use it as a compass for keeping on track at all times.

When you develop your strategic plan with this mission as your foundation, you'll find it to be not only a compass, but a roadmap that can take you clearly to your desired outcome of performance, financial strength, and growth. Remember that the Constitution of the United States of America is a mission statement that was written down by the framers in Philadelphia. This mission statement is the statement of purpose to serve "We the people...." and no matter how we have interpreted this document over time, it always represents nothing more than an idea brought to existence by people working together to develop and preserve it.

## Step 4 — The Development Process

I think there are two reasons to be in business or to work in a business, and they are, to have fun and make money, in that order. The pathway to a new or revised sales strategy is not long or arduous and will be a lot of fun if you start out with those thoughts in mind. A lot of human suffering happens when those two priorities are reversed, yet it is the way of the world for millions of workers and business owners.

Start out with a meeting of all the people listed above to present your metrics and research as they apply to your business and your customers. If you do not now measure your traffic, or know your true close ratio or average sale, you should perform a carefully planned study for at least two months prior to the meeting to accurately measure these key metrics. Without knowing your baseline metrics, you cannot set strategic goals for improvement, which should be the purpose of your sales strategy development process.

The first step is to gain consensus on the goals of this project:

» To produce more sales from the existing traffic base (assume no increase in traffic; instead look for improvement of metrics in your established traffic numbers)

» To improve the store close ratio to the specific level as calculated in your opportunity analysis

» To improve the store average sale to a specified level

» To improve the number of Be-Backs and return customers to a specific level (15 percent is a good first-step goal)

There can be more than these four, but I recommend that all members of your management team agree to these four because they are central to success. Remember this:

> **You cannot improve your sales. You can only improve the variable elements that make up your sales, opportunities, close ratio, and average sale.**

Once everyone agrees and understands that there are things you can do as a company to improve sales performance and profitability, you can simply ask for ideas. In these brainstorming meetings, there are no bad ideas and no foregone conclusions. Everything is up for grabs as it relates to how to improve the company's performance.

Here's a good, fun way to get ideas on the table and involve everyone from the beginning:

⟐ These are called "Idea Notes."

⟐ Someone acts as the facilitator – the idea gatherer.

⟐ Use banner paper (available in 26" or 30" rolls). Roll it out and pin to a wall a sheet about 15' long to resemble a blackboard.

⟐ Use 3" x 5" sticky-notes (and buy a lot of them) for people to write down ideas.

⟐ Have people write down three ideas (one per note) on how to capitalize on the research you've shown them. Have them use all the same color and no more than four words per note.

⟐ When done, have them, pass the notes to the facilitator, who reads and sticks them up on the banner paper in no particular order.

⟐ When they are all posted, assign another team member to group them like-to-like. You will find there are many duplicates.

⟐ Ask for explanations of the ideas from the group. The person(s) who put out certain ideas will explain his or her thoughts, but everyone can join in.

⟐ Combine like ideas, and cull out those that the group unanimously rejects (but hold on to them).

⟐ Have the group rank the remaining ideas by vote,

from the most likely to succeed to the least. There can be ties. The facilitator listens and rearranges. (You can also rank them by other criteria such as cost or time.)

This first step is the hardest and might take several hours or even as long a day. If you stop at this point, set an absolute time for the next session. If you keep the sessions short, you will have an easier time fitting them into people's busy schedules, and you'll hold people's attention more easily with shorter meetings.

For the second session, retain one sticky note for each of the ideas you decided to pursue.

» Put them up on the banner paper across the top so you can add sticky notes beneath them

» Ask everyone to write three sticky notes, four words each, about what resources you'll need to achieve each one of the ideas.

   » There are two types of resources: those you have and those you don't.
   » There are resources that require additional capital investment.
   » There are resources that require money from elsewhere.
   » There will be people requirements — manpower.
   » There will be cross-department training needed.
   » There will be expenditures outside just the sales department.
   » There will have to be accountability for performance.
   » There will be time requirements.
   » There will be training required.

Let these come from the group, and have your facilitator (it can be a different person for each meeting) put them in place as people complete them and hand them in. Hammer out the resources required to develop and implement each of the ideas for increasing sales based on your data and your research.

## Step 5 — Financial Accountability and Performance Metrics

Performance metrics provide you with easy ways to structure your strategic plan around financial data that are critical to your company's profitability. For example, if you have the sales metrics explained in Chapter 2, they will form your current baseline performance level. Your goals for sales revenue can then be calculated and become part of the strategic sales plan. For example:

Your door traffic for the baseline period was 10,000 customer opportunities over six months. Typically, that would mean that you'll see 20,000 opportunities in a year. If your close ratio for the same period was 20 percent, you'll make 4,000 sales, and if your average sale is $1,200, you'll write $4,800,000 in sales. Now, if your cancellation ratio (or drop-out rate) is 2 percent, you'll likely deliver and record as sales $4,704,000.

At 45 percent gross margin, you will have $2,116,800 to pay all your expenses and make a profit. I suggest you begin at the end and write in your net profit before taxes, let's say 10 percent or $470,400, now leaving you only $1,646,400 to pay expenses.

This little exercise in pure wishful thinking will stimulate a lot of creative thinking by you and your executive team. If your sales opportunity analysis shows that improving the performance of below average performers just to the average levels would improve your close ratio to 22.5 percent (a 10 percent increase), and your average sale to $1,320 (a 10 percent increase), then your delivered sales will be $5,940,000 (a 26.3 percent increase) giving you *$973,140 additional gross margin dollars.*

This substantial improvement will come about by simply, or not so simply, improving the performance of people through training, coaching, and management. You don't need any more customers than you're getting, and you don't have to spend any more ad dollars than you're spending IF you have a strategy, the right selling and management systems, and the will to make it happen one salesperson at a time. Remember, nearly half your salespeople are already performing at these levels.

### Sales Department Accountabilities for Performance

You can now summarize the sales department's accountabilities for achieving specific levels of financial performance, and you will do this kind of summary for each of the departments and department heads.

### Goals for the Sales Department

We began our strategic planning work with these goals:

» To produce more sales from the existing traffic base (here you have to assume no increase in traffic. If your traffic over the last six months was 10,000 shoppers, you should just look for improvement over your next 10,000 shoppers no matter the time span)
  » **We will to achieve the below performance levels over the next 10,000 customer opportunities.**
» To improve the store close ratio to the specific level as calculated in your opportunity analysis
  » **We will achieve a store close ratio of 22.5 percent.**
» To improve the store average sale to a specific level
  » **We will achieve a store average sale of $1,320.**
» To improve the number of Be-Backs and return customers to a specific level

> » **Be-Backs will be 15 percent of our customer opportunities**
- ❧ To improve overall sales to **$5,940,000**
- ❧ To maintain gross margin at **45 percent**

## Step 6 — Your Selling Strategy

Your strategy development team has come up with a list of things your company can do to capture those customers who shop but don't buy, and those who are struggling with the room design issues around their purchase decision. They believe that doing these things will achieve the goals they've established after analyzing the company's performance metrics

### Goal — Getting Connected and Staying Connected to Close Sales and Develop Be-Back Visits

You have to be "connected" in some meaningful way to that 10 percent to 15 percent of your customers who make their purchase the first time they shop in your store. Many things have to be right to get people to purchase big-ticket items. Because the close ratio on second-time shoppers is so high (75 percent or higher), your overall store closing ratio on customer visits will be between 18 percent and 22 percent if you change nothing you're doing. These are those "easy-to-sell" customers I talked about earlier.

What you need strategically is a way to connect to those customers who are not easy to sell, who need more help around the decorating issues before making their decision. If you don't provide this help, they will not become customers. There are as many customers in this group as in the "easy-to-sell" group, and in my experience, they also have more money to spend than the "easy-to-sell" group.

In order to improve your Be-Backs numbers, you have to do a better job of serving all your customers the first time they shop. You can't treat the "needs-more-help" customers the same way you treat the "easy-to-sell" customers, because that's what has produced your 20 percent close ratio. To get to 30 percent, to get that one more out of ten to buy, you have to provide more help to everyone.

Raising your level of service by always dealing with your customers' rooms as your way to understand their needs will likely improve the quality of all your sales, as salespeople sell more add-in items to the easy-to-sell group.

Here are some things your team might have come up with to address what you learned from your research and performance data and to achieve your goals for performance

» Redesign the selling system to include room-centered engagement strategies for salespeople to use with all their customers to offer more help in decision-making (a way to capture some of the 40 percent of uncertain customers)
  » Costs
    ▸ Hiring outside training company
    ▸ Follow-up retraining
» Ensure there is a Customer Relationship Management Program in place to track performance and provide salespeople with a follow-up system that can be observed and managed.
  » Costs
    ▸ System
    ▸ Hardware
    ▸ Installation
    ▸ Maintenance and support
» Develop a customer or room-planning profile form for salespeople to use to record customer information, including all contact information and email addresses. This is the controlling document for salespeoples' accountability for each prospective customer that they engage.

» Provide a place for room information, including sketches

» List all products and estimated retail prices

❧ Offer free design services to everyone who comes into your store. Hire or develop a staff designer to be available to customers through salespeople when there are obviously unresolved design issues to be dealt with. This has the potential to pay for itself quickly due to the new sales that will be generated.

❧ Compensate this staff designer at salary plus bonus. Allow her/him to develop relationships with private, outside designers to add additional revenue. Base bonuses on sales written by her, or in partnership with salespeople, for qualified room-planning projects that meet specific requirements.

» Costs

▸ Recruiting and hiring

▸ Designer salary and bonuses, payroll taxes and benefits

▸ Added responsibility for sales manager

▸ Performance tracking system

❧ Train all salespeople to be able to deliver basic room design services to all their customers who need that level of help. Make "more help" available to everyone who shops in your store at no additional charge.

» Costs

▸ Bringing in an outside trainer

▸ Developing and delivering your own training

▸ Added responsibility for sales managers

▸ Performance tracking system

❧ Purchase a room-planning software program for use by salespeople and customers on your selling floor, using multiple terminals throughout the showroom.

» Costs
  ▸ Software
  ▸ Hardware
  ▸ Installation
  ▸ Training
  ▸ Maintenance and support
❯ Develop an in-home design program that will serve qualified customers at no additional charge — a free service to generate a lot of additional business. This can be performed by the salesperson in partnership with the staff designer.
❯ Develop a sales budget for the year to account for all the costs and improved performance requirements.
  » Target the gains shown in the performance improvement analysis
    ▸ Sales improve to $5,940,000

## Other Departmental Strategies

The above process addresses the top line on your income statement, Sales, and also several expense categories such as salaries, benefits, and insurance. But you also have to account for all the other lines on your statement in two ways.

First, you have to maintain your target gross margin and GMROI, a responsibility of the merchandising and sales departments, requiring that you have a clear pricing strategy that everyone understands and is accountable for. While GMROI is not a line item on your income statement, most industry-specific computer systems track it and report it. GMROI is a critical performance metric for retailers.

Second, each department has to live within its expense budget as a percentage of sales. There are many guides for this in the home furnishings industry, the NHFA Annual Operating Report for retailers being one, and the *Furniture Today* Operating Report being another. These studies use results submitted by a number of companies and report the averages. In the NHFA report, companies are broken down as being either high profit or low profit. Again, when dealing with averages, which all these do, there is a range of performance within a group of companies that is not generally reported, but would be good to know (as you have seen in using sales metrics). Remember, another definition of average is, it's the best of the worst, but using averages for managing the range of performance in data is valuable. By reporting on the highest and lowest elements in their studies, reporting companies can help you understand the most desirable outcome, and you can see where your performance ranks along the line of performance results.

Using these reported numbers as a guide, along with your own actual results, you can develop a department-by-department list of key performance metrics to write into your strategic plan. Compare your results with the model in the studies, and continue your idea sessions to determine how each department can bring their numbers into line with the best performance model you can find in industry studies.

## Step 7 — Inventory and Cash Management

Because this book deals primarily with sales strategy, I won't expand on non-sales issues except for a brief discussion of inventory and GMROI. You must understand and manage GMROI to fulfill your goals for growth and profits and to do the one thing many retail store owners and managers fail to do — conserve cash. Cash is your lifeblood; inventory is death, the grim reaper, the cancer in too many home furnishings retail operations. The importance of this issue is demonstrated by:

> ❧ To optimize sales you must have your best selling items and groups in stock or readily available a very high percentage of the time. There

is a significant number of shoppers who will become buyers if you can give them what they want
quickly, because of the nature of the decisions to
buy that we discussed in Chapter 1.

❧ To continue to purchase these items and keep
them flowing, you must have cash reserves available. Reserves will not be available if you are heavy
in stock of poor selling goods. Being in a strong
cash position also makes it possible for you to take
advantage of many other business opportunities.
Advertising and promotional opportunities and developing a strong web presence and web site are
just a few that come to mind.

❧ The higher your special order ratio is to total sales,
the higher your overall GMROI should be, because
there is no inventory associated with these goods
aside from those that are in your warehouse waiting to be delivered to customers as your computer
system calculates average inventory. Finding the
right vendors to support your special order needs
in all categories of products is critical to success in
improving your GMROI.

Maintaining a high overall GMROI indicates that you
have a well-balanced inventory and should have cash on
hand to purchase what you need to keep generating even
more gross margin dollars. It means you do not have a lot
of slow-selling inventory that will only further diffuse your
GMROI due to heavy markdowns required to sell it — if you
can ever sell it.

Maintaining a high GMROI also means you will not have
to depend on bank credit to purchase inventory at high interest (to me, anything over 0 percent is high), thereby adding
expense to your income statement that would not be there if
your purchasing was based on measured factors instead of
buying deals that look good to you at a furniture show.

Pareto's Principle is very much in operation for furniture retailers. This is the law of imbalance and it states that a few causes produce most of the outcomes. You are subject to this statistical law in all areas of your business. You need to always be aware of which small portion of your items (groups) are providing the lion's share of your sales and profits, and you should invest your inventory dollars in the few and put no dollars into the many. It's really that simple, but it's not always easy.

GMROI answers the question, "How many gross margin dollars do I get back for every dollar I invest in inventory?" It is not an easy thing to calculate using cost-to-price numbers, because it represents the relationship between your inventory-turns over a measured time, and the gross margin dollars generated over that time. Whether you're tracking individual items or your total inventory, GMROI is the most crucial element in judging your financial performance. For our purposes, the targeted GMROI is the responsibility of your merchandisers and buyers, and is the most critical metric for which they are accountable.

As with sales, you cannot improve your GMROI by direct action, because it is a combination of several other factors that you can measure and improve, specifically stock levels and turns and gross margin. However, you cannot control gross margin if you are constantly forced to sell large amounts of goods at heavily discounted prices

## Step 8 — Document Your Strategic Plan

Keep your clean slate banner organized and visually understandable. One way to do this is to use different colors of sticky notes for different categories of information. For example, you might use the basic yellow colored notes for all of the first steps, then, use orange notes for things that require actual expenditure of dollars. Blue can be for those things that require new tasks for people to perform.

You can use different colors for actions to be taken by various departments or people. Your reason for doing this is to make documentation of the entire strategic process easier, because a strategic plan that is not written, widely distributed across the organization, and specific as to your goals and objectives for each department, employee, or group, is no plan at all.

You will write your plan using the Idea Notes as your outline. Using MS Word's headings hierarchy you can quickly build your outline using all of the key issues from your Idea Notes. You can expand on the ideas as you think it is necessary for clarity and to explain complex points, but don't make the final document too lengthy, keep your descriptions as short as possible to be understood. Your company strategic sales plan can now be distributed throughout the company.

This is not to say that every employee has to have access to every aspect of your plan. At the executive level, and for department heads in larger companies, the need to know is great and the benefits of opening financial results are huge. In most family companies, these things are too often kept secret, thereby undoing accountability for performance down through the organization. This is usually a bad thing.

For each department, however, I strongly urge you review with the group and each individual worker the overall plan, and provide details about the plan for their department. It is important to know that employees understand the role they play, and how the results of their work contribute to the company's overall success. (In Part Three, you'll learn how you can assure individual accountability for performance at all levels of your company, and ensure that you achieve your strategic mission, goals, and objectives.)

There are three reasons for writing your plan down. First is to ensure that all executives have a clearly written agreement on what is required from their areas in terms of productivity and accountability; department heads are accountable for achieving goals and objectives in their area of responsibility. The written plan will form the agenda for all future meetings of the executive and management teams relative to how you're doing.

Second is to be sure you communicate down the organization in a way that doesn't jeopardize the security of private financial information but that shows individuals what is required from them to achieve company goals for revenue, expenses, and profitability. I use the term profitability instead of profits because it has the connotation of long-term performance. By doing this you are telling your employees that if they do their jobs as laid out in their job descriptions, living up to all performance metrics that apply to them, their share of the accountability for performance will be achieved. Profitability is an important concept in that it predicts profits into the future.

## Step 9 — The Standards of Performance Defined and Documented

The third reason for having a written plan is that for all areas of your business where performance metrics are available, and there are a lot of them, this document clearly spells out the standards of expected performance for all key managers. In our sales department example, the key required outcomes are clear because there are, first of all, just those three elements to deal with (opportunities, close ratio, and average sales).

These published standards of performance become the driving force behind the selling strategies that we'll develop in Part Two, and provide the desired outcome for that process when coupled with the consumer research that we covered in Chapter 1. In Chapter 4, you'll see how to define and document specific behaviors, work processes, and selling dialogs for the entire sales process that will then be made into detailed training materials to form the training and coaching foundation for all salespeople.

# PART TWO

*The Selling System*

*Developing Your
Customer Engagement
Strategy*

# INTRODUCTION TO PART TWO

In every sales seminar I've ever presented to salespeople and sales managers, I have asked the group this question: "What is the first furniture item a woman shops for when she's planning to do her living room or family room over?" Nearly 100 percent of the time, the answer is "a sofa." I then ask this question: "Is a sofa ever the very last thing they buy?" The answer is always, "No." My reply is, "Well now, think about this: If you have a customer who is shopping for a sofa, and you sell her a sofa, you feel good about making that sale, but how connected are you to the rest of the room? How connected are you to her decorating project?" These lost opportunities for selling more to some customers, particularly relational types, are critically important to you as business owners, managers, and salespeople

The success or failure of your business strategy comes down to how the people who meet and serve your customers deliver that strategy to the customer. All the strategic planning in the world is meaningless if the people on the front line don't execute the plan.

I've been in hundreds of stores across America and dealt with thousands of managers and salespeople spreading the message you'll see unfold in the following chapters. There is no doubt in my mind that, while there is huge opportunity for improvement, there is also a huge need for sensible training and on-the-spot coaching by sales managers.

Most salespeople are disconnected from the true, deep-rooted needs of many customers they face. The cost to your company of not reacting to these performance issues can easily be as high as 25 percent of sales. This represents the sales you don't make to people who shop in your store, who could buy (they have the money), should buy (you have things they like), but don't buy because they need more help regarding how your products will solve their room-centered decorating problems, or because of poor sales, closing, and follow-up skills. Additionally, there are lost sales to customers who do buy from you, but who really need, and would buy, much more.

It is this idea about connecting to customer's decorating projects that form the foundation for what follows in this part of this book.

So far in this book I've shown you some of the consumer research supporting my view, dealt with the issues of how to use your own results (metrics) to know where improvement is possible and necessary, and how you can bring all the tremendous resources of intelligence and creativity within your employees to bear on developing a solution. In this part, we'll deal with developing one possible strategic solution, which is one of many possible strategies.

## Three Retail Home Furnishings Models

I believe there are three distinctly different, broad strategic approaches to selling furniture through traditional type locations, where furniture and home furnishings are the only products offered for sale. They are:

- ❧ Big-Box or large regional chains
- ❧ Independents
- ❧ Branded stores

## 1. Big-Box and Large Regional Chains

First is the strategy of most "big box" retailers and regional chains. This is a smart strategy that sells a lot of furniture, but requires huge resources usually not available to smaller, independent retailers, and top-notch systems in every area of the business.

These are some of the common traits of these companies:

- ❧ They are well financed and managed, and may be primarily in the business of creating valuable real estate wealth.
- ❧ They are gross margin-driven.
- ❧ They own most or all of their store locations.
- ❧ They manage their inventory and cash flow moment-by-moment and control their expenses.
- ❧ They turn their inventory more quickly than average industry retailers to generate higher GMROI.
- ❧ They have detailed sales and operating budgets.
- ❧ They demand accountability for performance at all levels.
- ❧ Their stores are well located and displayed.
- ❧ They monitor their product lineup sales performances daily against strict performance requirements.
- ❧ All purchases must pass a financial test for open-to-buy and meet strict financial guidelines. The people who buy things deal with the *art* of merchandising, while financial people deal with the *science* of merchandising.
- ❧ They maintain large central inventories of everything they display, and deliver quickly. This is their main selling proposition.

- » They saturate discrete markets with locations and leverage their advertising dollars to be the most pervasive home furnishings force in their markets, driving enormous numbers of consumers through their doors.
- » They staff their selling floors to higher levels than required to account for high traffic levels and to minimize the effects of poor individual performance.
- » They are not interested in incurring the costs of individual training and development of salespeople beyond initial training on systems, products.
- » There is a high level of management presence on the selling floor at all times. These positions may be expanded sales positions targeted at closing sales, which makes up for some of the weaknesses of poor-performing salespeople. These people may be titled Floor Managers or Sales Managers.
- » They accept high sales employee turnover and recruit constantly and aggressively.
- » They use selling tactics that target their revenue needs — tactics such as high levels of product knowledge, in stock for immediate delivery, selling whole rooms as shown instead of just items, and long-term financing with no money down.
- » They maintain extensive customer lists, both internally generated and purchased, and use direct marketing to the max.

The above list of business traits has elements that should be true of all retailers in the home furnishings industry, specifically those points concerning financial and inventory management. Others are not feasible for small, independent retailers to achieve because they are characteristic of large, multi-location companies where economies of scale are in place. In most cases, these regional companies have grown into their markets slowly, one location at a time, on a planned and carefully executed basis. Their size and financial strength allow them to offer financing to their customers on terms that are simply not available to small companies.

## 2. Independent Retailers

These are single or multiple-location, family-owned companies. many of which are multi-generational and are now in the second or third generation of ownership. They may operate stores in more than one community in a region.

Given the above listed characteristics of the large regional companies, it might appear that small, independent companies might as well roll over and die. However, I believe there are ways to survive and thrive in competition with these giants because I know that their metrics aren't any different from those I've shown in Chapter 2. What is different is that the large regional companies get so many more customers through their doors that they can generate the revenue they need to produce the gross margin they need even on mediocre performance by their salespeople. The fact is though, that, just as with all furniture stores, many of their salespeople are terrific performers and some are not.

Independents generally have tried to set themselves apart from the big regional or national chains through higher service and better quality merchandise. They also place a lot of emphasis on the family-owned aspect, the "local" aspect, and the longevity issue. They generally don't try to compete on price or stock availability with their larger counterparts. When these smaller retailers are well managed and have the right systems in place to operate their businesses, and when they constantly strive to provide a defined higher level of service at all levels, they can succeed. To remain profitable and grow in both good times and bad, these retailers have to:

❧ Maintain low inventories and conserve cash at all costs.

❧ Keep their best-selling merchandise in stock and on order in reasonable quantities relative to current sales requirements. They must not sit on even good selling merchandise for long periods. The cost of carrying an item in inventory for one year is approximately 30 percent of its cost.

❧ Move their poor selling inventory out of stock and display quickly at the highest possible margins — this means they must have a markdown strategy to recognize and move out their "dogs."

❧ Maintain profitable gross margin while clearly recognizing that all expenses and profits are dependent only on gross margin dollars, and that is where their attention should be directed.

❧ Organize to minimize expenses to ensure profitability while not cutting back on any critical functions that will have a reverse affect on company performance.

❧ Make maximum use of all computer systems to keep personnel costs low. Let the computer system run the company operations and the people run the system.

❧ Optimize sales by controlling the point of contact with the customer throughout the entire customer engagement with a selling strategy and system that connects them to each customer, whether transactional or relational, in a way superior to their bigger competitors.

❧ Maintain sales management presence on the selling floor at all times. Take all administrative duties off the list of sales managers' tasks. Sales management is performance management.

❧ Offer in-store and in-home room planning and design solutions to all customers at no added cost to them. This is the elusive "more help" that is required to get that one more shopper out of ten to buy.

» Involve their salespeople in the processes of bringing customer opportunities into the store through an active, formal, computer-based customer follow-up strategy and system.

» Demonstrate accountability for performance at all levels of their company, but particularly at the executive or department head level.

» Provide more help to those customers who need it and want it. This is the primary area where independents can take customers from their competition and improve customer loyalty and satisfaction.

» Develop or upgrade their websites by making it easy for customers to shop online, including finance applications, full product displays with pictures, and pricing. This is the first place that ad dollars should be spent until it is right. More shoppers will find them here than anywhere else.

» Provide the highest level of delivery and other after-the-sale services by training all delivery and service personnel to be the final link in the selling strategy chain of performance.

### 3. Branded Stores — Company-Owned and Independently Owned

Included in this group are Ethan Allen, La-Z-Boy, Thomasville, Lane, Drexel-Heritage, Bassett, and other stores operating under a manufacturer's brand. Virtually all of these types of stores operate as licensees of the manufacturer and are not franchises. Nearly all of these networks include stores owned by private individuals or families (licensees) and stores owned and operated by the manufacturer.

Historically, only Ethan Allen did this right. They have no other distribution channels to compete with their stores.

If you want to buy Ethan Allen furnishings, you have to go to an Ethan Allen store. They are, therefore, the most successful and profitable of these types of stores.

The issues with this model are many and varied. Some independent owners have done spectacularly well when they have been able to meld one or more of these stores with their regular furniture business to achieve economies of scale. Others have failed miserably, and it is beyond the scope of this book to detail the reasons why.

## All Types of Stores Benefit

Each of these three types of stores can benefit from what you'll read here in terms of improving sales revenue. No matter how well you're doing, if you're not doing these things, you are not maximizing your potential to do business. The customers I'm talking about, who have shopped, but have not purchased have already been in your store. They're still out there with their need unsatisfied, but if you don't know who they are, don't have their names and contact information, and your salesperson didn't earn the right to follow up with them, only your advertising can bring them back.

However, since they already were in your store, dealt with one of your salespeople, and didn't buy, why should they come back for more of the same? If they need more help and you can't provide it, why go through that again? Moreover, if your selling strategy involves attempting to "overcome objections" and a customer is in the dreaming or exploring stages of her decision-making process, you're likely off the shopping list completely.

The things you think work for you only work for that group of more transactional customers, the customers I call "easy-to-sell" – somewhere around 20 to 25 percent of the total number who shop with you. Your immediate opportunity for more sales is to change the way you work with customers from the old-time methods of show-and-tell to a new, higher level of service and get one more customer out of every ten to buy from your store. This is the message of the next chapter in the strategic development of your selling strategy.

SECRETS TO
ENGAGING
CUSTOMERS

## Introduction

I consider every furniture or home furnishings purchase made by a customer to be a part of a project. Women don't shop for things in an intellectual or decorating vacuum. Everything they buy is part of some home decorating or room design project they're working on. Sometimes you meet them at the beginning, and sometimes in the middle or at the end. Sometimes the project has been going on for a very long time — months, or even years. It's important to find out what her project, and where she is in the process of completing it.

If you meet her at the beginning of her project, in the dreaming or exploring stages, consider yourself very lucky, because you can become a trusted advisor and friend as long as you connect to the person and her project. However, you have to be very careful in how you deal with her, because if your engagement strategy is based only on making a sale today, you risk turning her off and being scratched off her shopping list. If she's in the middle stage of planning, you still have a great opportunity to connect. If you meet her at the end, and she's shopping for "finishing touch" items, you can set yourself up for the next project, because there will be one.

## Room Design Profiles — Salesperson Accountability

The first step in building an active customer base[*] is a document I call a Room Design Profile. This is used to record all of information about every customer engaged, no matter how much or how little information is obtained: contact information, a record of all the products they expressed interest in, and a sketch of the room (which I discuss in detail in the next chapter).

Room Design Profiles also give you a hard copy of your contact with customers that you can file and use outside of the computer-based CRM system, when your customers return for appointments. All your information will be there to refresh your memory and serve your customer. See the Appendices for a sample Room Design Profile form.

There another good reason to use this form: It provides accountability to the management. In our kind of one-to-one, personal selling, where you represent the business owner as an agent of the company, you owe an accounting for each customer opportunity you are assigned. In addition, tracking your personal opportunities is important to your immediate manager, because it is his or her responsibility to guide you in achieving your personal goals for sales and income. In order to do this, she needs to know everything about your success equation (Sales = Customer Opportunities x Close Ratio x Average Sale). Your Room Design Profile is the vehicle you'll use to ensure that you enter every customer's information into your Customer Relationship Management system after each engagement. Room Design Profiles are a coaching tool for review with your coaches and managers to ensure you are on track with the selling strategy.

---

[*] In Chapter 8 I discuss the issue of maintaining an active customer base as being critical to your success. I believe this is one thing that many salespeople in our industry are very poor at doing and that, if you use it well, has a greater effect on your success than any other factor.

## Your Strategic Foundation

We've all heard that when meeting someone for the first time you have 10 seconds to make an impression — good or bad. I think that's reasonably accurate, so let's look at what we know about our customers and develop a way to engage them that considers all of our experience and research.

» All customers are involved in a project of some kind, even those transactional shoppers.
» All of your customers are in one of the five stages of decision making:
  » Dreaming
  » Exploring
  » Planning
  » Selection
  » Enjoyment
» A very large percentage of first-time shoppers on a home furnishings project (I say as many as 90 percent) **will not** make a purchase on their first visit. Therefore, if you handle 10 customer opportunities today, and they're all first-time shoppers on a project, you might make one sale.
» If this is a return customer, then you will make a sale over 70 percent of the time. It doesn't matter whether the customer is more transactional or relational — the second time is the charm.
» Of these customers, 41 percent of customer opportunities are unable to see the end result they want and are confused about design. These are the same group who said they shopped but didn't buy — *they need more help.*

How should you approach these customers? Here are some essential strategies:

❧ You have to deal with this person in such a way that you make a great first impression, show sincere interest in them and their project, develop a relationship of trust and competence, and earn the right to follow up with them to bring them back.

❧ You have to find out about the customer's project. You need to know what it is they are trying to accomplish. *You need to see the picture your customer has in her mind of her room today and in the future.* This is true for both transactional and relational type shoppers. Transactional shoppers are price-sensitive, but are not insensitive to the design issues around their purchase. The information to find out is:

» Why are they making this change?

» How long have they been shopping?

» What is the extent of the changes they're considering?

» What is staying in the room?

» Will there be changes in flooring, walls, and window treatments?

» When do they want it to be completed?

» What are they expecting to spend to accomplish their goal?

» How long have they been shopping for this?

» What's the most important element in their decision-making?

❧ You have to know everything she knows about the room they're working on, such as:

» What other rooms are affected?

» What about color flow between rooms or areas?

» How do they use this room?

» Size, shape, light...remember, she knows the room completely, and you know nothing about it at all.

» You have to understand the decorating or design issues they're struggling with:
  » What look or feel do they want for the room?
  » What will make her say, when it's all done, "I love this room"?
» Finally, your company has to have a way to help all customers who get more help who need it:
  » Room planning software on your website and in your stores is absolutely necessary to help customers answer simple questions around size, fit, and room layout.

I believe that every furniture store should have a staff designer, or room-planning specialist, who can assist salespeople and customers with questions and advice around room layout, color coordination, accessorizing rooms, style selection, window treatments, and all other issues related to using our products. This is how we fulfill our stated mission.

The staff designer can also be in charge of store display, certain purchasing under the guidelines of merchandising management. If you cannot offer some level of room planning to your customers, however, you are not optimizing your customers' experiences in your store, and your results will be what they have always been, except less.

## Your Greeting Agenda

For three decades, I've observed thousands of customer greetings and engagements on hundreds of selling floors across America. There are two kinds of approaches that salespeople use. One works, and the other fails.

When I look at performance data regarding sales success is situations where I know the people involved, I usually see that those with the best social (interpersonal) skills — are above average and those with the worst perform below average. My observation is that it begins with a smile and a welcoming "Hello" in the first few seconds.

» If your agenda is to sell, you will be moderately successful, but only average at best.
» If your agenda is to understand first, then to help solve problems, you'll succeed, and enjoy your work a lot more.

Your first and most important goal when greeting any customer has to be to connect to them through polite and service-based dialog, and to get to the point where you can make this request:

**"Tell me about your room."**

This simple request is the real point of connection and engagement for you with all shoppers, transactional or relational. For transactional types, the final decision may be influenced by price, but the issues they face up to that point are the same as for relational shoppers. This is when your customer will open up and talk about her decorating problems and needs. This is the point where, unlike telling her all about your store and your products, the engagement becomes all about her, her home, her room, and her issues. The sooner you can get to the point where you can ask your customer to do this, the sooner you'll be on your way to a successful engagement.

"Tell me about your room" is simply the magic request in our world. It works nearly every time to get people talking about the real issues they're facing, and sets you up to be a consultant, a friend in the business; when you use the information you receive to understand before you use it to sell, you have begun a trusting relationship with your customer.

You can't just ask this of a customer, however, without interacting on an interpersonal level first. You have to **earn** *the right* to ask that she share personal information with you, and your request has to be made in the context of her needs. This chapter will show you how to get to that point.

Eventually, selling always comes down to closing the sale, and you have to have those skills, but it's easier to use your closing skills when you are fully aligned with your customer's true needs and have gained her trust by connecting to her and her quality-of-life issues around her project.

## Put on a Happy Face

If you can't go to the door with a smile to greet your next customer, you're in the wrong field of work. Selling home furnishings is fun. Customers are fun, but because of their experiences in retail furniture stores, and the confusion, uncertainty and fear they have around making the right choice, they often appear to be reticent and withdrawn. Nothing succeeds like a sincere smile and a pleasant "Hello, welcome."

If the first ten seconds are important, the first instant is more important. An unsmiling salesperson doesn't give a reticent customer many reasons to relax and actually *feel* welcome, or to believe that this salesperson is himself a happy person eager to understand *their* problem, *their* issues, and *their* needs. If you look and act like someone whose day has been interrupted by this intrusion, you're not going to connect very well with many customers.

When salespeople complain to me about the "mean" nature of customers, how standoffish they are, or how rude they are, I always spend some time observing them in actual customer engagements. Not surprisingly, in most cases the customer's reaction is a mirror of the salesperson's demeanor on approaching the customer. The problem is that these salespeople don't think their demeanor is off-track at all.\*

I've seen and used dozens of greetings in my work over the decades in training salespeople and developing selling

---

\* Dealing with this problem is the topic of Chapter 13 in Part Three systems. I've concluded that it's not so much the words you say, but how you say them that matters. People pick up immediately on the "vibes" that others generate. It's up to you to emotionally and mentally be in the right place inside yourself when you meet a customer. This is, after all, the way you earn your living.

You can get yourself into the right frame of mind by thinking of your work as being much more than just selling furniture, or whatever your products are. The business you are in helps people achieve outcomes that are far more important to them than you might think. Beautiful rooms and homes are basic to the quality of life of the people you serve. It's never just about furniture; it goes far beyond that.

When you are working with a dining room customer, showing and explaining the features of the items, you have to know the picture in her mind. For many Americans, that picture is of one or two days in the entire year — Thanksgiving and Christmas or Passover for many. The picture is a family picture; there are feelings connected to this picture, and you must understand this, and believe it.

Couples shopping for a child's bedroom actually see their child using the furniture, not just the appearance of the furniture. It's the outcome for your customer you need to be able to share with them and speak to, not just the features of the products or the details of the transaction.

Customers shopping for family room furniture see their families actually using the room: Relaxing, reclining, watching sports or movies together, and having fun. It is these feelings that your selling efforts need to promote. The furniture is secondary to these feelings and images of comfort, beauty, and security. This is not to say that the furniture isn't important in and of itself. People buy things they like, things that are aesthetically pleasing to them and that match their innate sense of beauty, things that are comfortable. You cannot change this view in other people's minds.

You can only sell what you have or have access to through catalogs.

Remember our suggested mission:

**To help our customers understand how to use our products to enhance the comfort and beauty of their homes and their quality of life, not just how to buy them.**

Thinking about your work in this way will help you in every aspect of your work. You have to be sincere. You have to truly care about fulfilling your mission every time you smile and say hello to a new customer.

### How You Say Hello Is More Important than You Think

Just smile brightly and say this:

*"Hello. Welcome. How may I help you?"*

You don't have to insert your store's name. Your customers know where they are — really, they do. You don't have to use any other questions either, but if "how may I help you" sounds too old-time and worn out, you could ask:

*"What brings you in today?"*

If you have a greeting that is successful in connecting you to your customers every time and doesn't cause them to run back out the door, use it. If your close ratio is above the store average, and you have many Be-Back customers every month, don't change what you're doing. If you're satisfied with your earnings every week, month, and year, don't change a thing you do. If these qualifications don't apply to you, if you're stuck in a rut around connecting to customers, and your earnings are flat and not what you want, then you have nothing to lose by making a change to the things you're doing.

## Open-Ended Questions

Every book on sales and selling has to have the obligatory section on open questions. We also call them the "journalist's questions" because they have this in common: They cannot be answered "Yes" or "No." People have to offer expansive answers. These questions always begin with one of the following words: Who, What, When, Where, Why, and How. Open questions are important to get your customers talking, but your purpose for using them cannot be to "get to the point" so you can begin showing them furniture.

Your agenda has to be one of understanding, not selling. You are a problem-solver, and before you can solve a problem, you have to understand it from your customer's point of view. You cannot successfully offer a solution to a problem you do not understand; therefore your first goal has to be to know more about them, their room, and their needs.

## Make It All About Them

Your simple greeting, "How may I help you?" is certainly about them. You are trying to find out what you need to know to help this customer solve her problem — a lot about their room and what they're trying to accomplish in it. There are two possible things customers will tell you when they're shopping for furniture:

1.  What it is they're shopping for
2.  That they're just looking

I find that the issue of the "I'm just looking" type of customer is far overstated by many salespeople and managers. Most people want help from a qualified professional who knows all about the products and services offered by your store. They don't have time to spend looking aimlessly around for things.

There is, of course, one notable exception: those women who are in the dreaming and exploring stages of their decision-making on a project. They truly are just looking, they truly are just "looking for *ideas*," and you can make customers out of them later if you do the right things now. If you do the wrong things now they'll simply not come back because your products and services, your displays and items, really aren't all that much different from your competitor's.

## Handling the "I'm just looking" Customer

I don't want you to try to break through the barrier of "I'm just looking." I believe that if you try to sell something to women in the early stages of a project and don't respect their space, you will lose them on this project. They will not give you a second chance.

For those people who are just afraid of being sold and interrogated by retail salespeople in furniture stores, or any store, you can't "overcome" this by acting in the same way that other salespeople have acted. Let them go.

> *"Terrific! This is a great place to look for ideas. Please enjoy our store. May I check in with you in a few minutes?"*

This idea of asking for permission is important to our goal of connecting to a customer by way of her home decorating problem and project. It is also an ongoing thread that weaves through this entire selling strategy. Always allow your customer to be in charge of what happens to her in your store until she is ready to engage you regarding her purpose for being in your store.

The idea of overcoming customer objections is an old-time selling concept that has been taught by sales trainers for decades. It's the wrong way to think about the issue of dealing with the customer's fear of being sold, uncertainty, lack of trust, lack of knowledge, and confusion. The right way to think about it in the context of retail home furnishings stores is that you have to talk and act in a way that builds trust, reduces fear, shows interest in her issues, and offers help. (You'll read more on how to handle customer feedback later in Chapter 6.)

When you do re-engage the browsing customer, be prepared to say something smart. I am always amazed at how little pre-engagement planning salespeople do, and I've observed some very weak and unsatisfactory re-engagement dialogs that actually hurt the salesperson's attempts to connect to a browsing customer. Here are some rules for re-engaging customers whom you've set free to browse:

- ❧ Don't wait too long – 5 to 8 minutes is enough.
- ❧ Ask customer-centered questions.
- ❧ "How are you enjoying our store?" Keep it about them.
- ❧ "What room are you working on?"
- ❧ Don't try to zero in on something you see her looking at. People looking for ideas will check out many different things in your store. Don't assume anything, and don't "pounce."
- ❧ Be polite, keep smiling, and remove all the pressure from your customer. Just act as though you were meeting a friend of a friend for the first time. Let her ask questions or volunteer information regarding her project.
- ❧ If she responds by telling you why she's shopping, proceed as explained in Chapter 5, "The Pathway to Understanding."

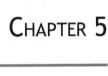

## THE PATHWAY TO UNDERSTANDING

### When They Tell You What They Want

The customer who tells you what she wants, either when you first meet her or after you re-engage her, has decided to trust you enough to open up her needs to you — a salesperson. How dangerous for her. You now have an opportunity to do all the right things based on what you know about your store's customers and customers in general.

Let's say your customer tells you that she's looking for a sofa. You know that this is the first item women shop for when they're making a major change in their room. They want to find the biggest single item that anchors the color plan and the rest of the room.

Begin like this:

*"Oh great! We have over one hundred sofas on display in every style and price range. I'm sure we'll find one that's just right for your room."*

*"To help me to better understand, tell me about your room."*

As she begins to explain, say:

**"Let me get this on paper."**

At this point, do the one thing that is more important than any other action you can take:

### Sketch the room.

Sketching the room is the physical activity that allows you to make your customer engagement completely about her and her room, her needs, and her decorating problems. Nothing you can do is more important for any customer, but especially for the large number of women who need more help with their room design project. Sketching a room with a customer is your great connector to her, personally, and to her room. This is the moment of connection.

Remember this important fact when you think about sketching: people think in pictures, not in words. Your customer has a complete picture of her room in her mind. She knows everything about it. She knows where everything is, what other rooms open into this room, where all the windows and doors are, how much outside light exists, and what the room looks like day and night. She knows everything, except probably the actual size, and you know, well, nothing.

You have to get that picture out of her head and into yours, and there are only two ways of doing this: Asking questions and rendering a sketch, or going to her home to see the room with her. Right now, sketching is the only way you have to see that picture.

You also will use the room sketch to connect the items you present to a place in the room.

After you've asked your customer to tell you about her room, let her begin talking, then politely interrupt and say this:

*"Let me put this on paper, it's much better when we can see it together."*

## Asking the Right Questions — Working With the Answers

Remember all the things you now have to do:

- ✦ You have to find out about the customer's project. You need to know what it is she is trying to accomplish.
  - » Who uses the room and how?
  - » Why is she making this change?
  - » How long has she been shopping?
  - » What is the extent of the changes she's considering?
  - » What is staying in the room?
  - » Will there be changes in flooring, walls, and/or window treatments?
  - » When does she want it to be completed?
  - » What is she expecting to spend to accomplish her goal?
- ✦ You have to know everything she knows about the room she's working on, such as:
  - » What other rooms are affected?
  - » What about color flow between rooms or areas?
  - » How do they use this room?
  - » Size, shape, light ... remember, she knows the room completely, and you know nothing about it at all.
- ✦ You have to understand the decorating or design issues she's struggling with.
  - » What look or feel does she want for the room?
  - » What will make her say, when it's all done, "I love this room"?

» You have to deal with the customer's comfort zone around price; this is the number one cause of failure in home furnishings selling:

» "Have you thought about what you want to spend for this?"

» "Tell me what price range you're thinking about."

When your customer doesn't have a budget, or isn't clearly seeking a specifically priced item, you have an opportunity to help her determine what's right for her. Price is one reason people do not buy on their early visits to stores. They're scouting styles, color, fabrics, fashion, price, and quality. You can connect at this point by being open, honest, and knowledgeable.

When your customer isn't sure of the outcome she is looking for, or expresses frustration around the process of determining that, you have a potential candidate for room-planning project work.

Learn this list of questions by heart. Ask them in a warm, friendly, conversational tone of voice — like a helpful, knowledgeable friend, not like a salesperson. The role you play can be either salesperson-like, or just person-to-person. Person-to-person is always better.

## Tips on Sketching

You don't have to be an artist to sketch a room. Follow these simple steps and you'll soon learn how easy it is to do. Remember this, sketching for understanding is not art. You are simply trying to understand better your customer's problem in order to help her solve it. Neatness does not count. Roughness is just fine. Take no more than five minutes to do this.

» Try to begin by sketching the outline of a rectangle. Most rooms are rectangular in basic form. Some will have other rectangles attached, such as for living room/dining room combinations, or bedroom/sitting area, etc. If the room is not a rectangle, let the customer tell you.

> » Some customers will know the dimensions of their rooms, but many will not. It is possible to determine approximate room size from the layout of the current furniture and the right questions.

❧ Get down the locations of all doors, entryways, and windows.

> » Ask what rooms this room opens to.
> » Determine which walls are half walls, or where there may not be any wall at all (such as from kitchens to family areas).

Sometimes your customer will ask for your pen and fill in the room themselves. Let them do it no matter how unclear it may be to you. You can fix it all later. The important thing is that when your customer does this, it shows you how important it is to her that you understand her room. Most people are happy that you've asked them about it and are anxious to share the picture in their head with you.

Many salespeople fear sketching, but my experience is that this is the most effective sales tool you have provided you use the information you get from it correctly.

❧ Sketch all current furniture in the room. To make sure you cover everything, it's a good idea to work around the room from one corner. Then ask the customer again, "What do you want to accomplish in this room?"

> » You will need to make another sketch, or more, to show the room the way they want it to be, or to offer suggestions around possible layouts.

» Ask questions as you sketch from the list above.

When you complete this much, stop. Say to your customer:

***"OK, let me be sure I understand."***

Now, review quickly but clearly. Feed back everything the customer told you about her room, her family, her likes and dislikes around styles and colors, and ask if you correctly understand everything. If she answers "yes," proceed to show her some furniture. This shows you paid attention while she talked. Start with this:

***"I've got some ideas. Do you have a budget or spending plan for the room?"***

***"I can help you with your budget. We have a range of prices in sofas, and I'll explain everything to you as we go."***

***"May I show you some things I think might work for you and get your feedback?"***

This will help you avoid making a big mistake at this point in your engagement. You need to understand the customer's budget issues.

At this point in your engagement with your customer, it's wise to move directly to product. Your company's selling strategy offers three levels of service for you to suggest to customers, but this is not the time for that unless your customer directly asks you about design services. It's preferable to get some feedback from your customer now and understand her likes and dislikes and her level of uncertainty.

By now, from her answers to your open-ended questions while sketching her room, you will have a good idea about the nature and scope of her project. You'll know whether there is reason to offer more help to this customer, or to close this sale today. You can always make the offers later in your relationship.

In the next chapter, you'll read why total product knowledge is so important to success in our industry, second only to knowledge of your customer, and understand how to go about learning all you need to know.

You have to know everything about everything you sell. That sounds like a tall order, but think about the foolishness of a salesperson selling things about which they know little or nothing. More important, customers expect you to know everything about your products, but in most research I've seen, customers' biggest complaint about salespeople is that they don't know a lot about their products.

In the make-believe example we have been following, you are now in a part of the customer engagement where you have to know quickly what to show your customer in order to judge the efficacy of your choices. Product knowledge is extremely important now.

Our business is unlike any other retail segment because there are so many suppliers, and so many versions of every product that the number of details a salesperson has to know, or know how to find, number in the tens of thousands. How can you deal with this avalanche of information?

## How Adults Learn

First, there's a difference between teaching (training) and learning. Teaching is the responsibility of teachers, trainers, or managers. Every sales manager's job description I've ever seen contains something about training salespeople. If the training is there, then it becomes a matter of learning, and that is the responsibility of the student, or employee.

Learning, in our context, means that salespeople exhibit new behaviors and offer enhanced product knowledge to customers. Learning has occurred when behavior on the floor changes.

You learn by receiving new information that you believe is important to you — to achieving your goals — and use it in your interactions with customers to close sales.

The learning process goes something like this:

» You receive new information, such as dialogs and selling methods like sketching rooms.
» You watch someone who is good at it, like a trainer or teacher, perform it.
» You practice the new skill in a controlled environment — you sketch coworkers' rooms just as you would with a customer.
» You perform with a customer, perhaps while being observed by a manager or coworker.
» If you succeed, you continue to perform your new skill under coaching by your manager and others.
» If you fail, you take additional training and practice, and go back at it again.
» You perform again with a customer, and provide feedback to your coach or manager.
» After performing successfully several times, and being coached through the process, you have effectively learned a new skill.

Adults get involved in the learning process because they believe the information is important to them. This holds for learning about products, too. In this regard, you need an overview of the company's merchandising plan. That is the role of the owner, buyer, sales manager, or merchandise manager. These people are responsible for implementing the company's merchandise strategy that includes vendor selection, item selection, pricing, and promotions.

## The Learning Plan

Your management staff will provide an overview of the company's merchandise strategy, giving you the price/quality overview based on the target audience your company serves. You already know what room-based product categories you sell, and if you're a full-line, multi-vendor company, you'll have living and family room upholstered furniture, occasional tables, and other items in the occasional genre. You have bedroom and bedding, dining room, kitchen/dining, youth, entertainment, home office, and accent or accessory furniture. That's pretty much the whole house. Accessories add a myriad of additional items to know about, but general information is good enough for that category.

You'll learn the range of pricing your store sells in each category. Some pricing will be by item (sofas and sectionals), and some by group (bedrooms and dining rooms). Your store may price upholstery groups as well as individual items, and you need to know the range from opening price points to the top of the line in order to serve your customers well.

People learn best by category. They also learn best when faced with a challenge that involves them with the merchandise, the catalogs, and the price lists. You will have Salespeople learn products best by category, not by vendor. Vendor representative training, which has its place, but the main job for vendor reps is to teach salespeople how to use their company's price lists and catalogs when special orders are allowed, and to know the quality aspects of the product's construction. Armed with the knowledge of your vendors and their quality features, it's time to hit the floor to become involved with every product in your store by category. Use a form like the Room Design Profile form provided in the Appendices to record all the information you can find about each product or group you encounter. Work only by category according to this list:

- ❧ Upholstered furniture
    - » Cloth-covered upholstery
    - » Leather-covered upholstery (leather/cloth combinations can be in either group or in a subgroup)
    - » All motion upholstery, including reclining sofas, chairs, and sleepers
- ❧ Occasional and accent furniture, including bars and game tables
- ❧ Bedroom furniture — master and adult bedrooms
- ❧ Youth furniture
- ❧ Entertainment furniture, wall systems, cabinets, specialized
- ❧ Dining room, kitchen, and dining room
- ❧ Home office
- ❧ Sleep sets

I suggest you don't make any style breakouts, but work one category at a time to completion before moving on to another category. Your goal is to learn everything you can about each group and item on your store's selling floor. You'll need to know the price point of each upholstered group (sofa, loveseat, chair, ottoman), bedroom group (bed, dresser, mirror, nightstand, chest), and dining group (table, chairs, china base and top) as well as the individual price point of the key items, such as sofas, sectionals, beds, and tables with chairs.

Your store may group differently and your trainer/manager will guide you in these matters, but the important thing for you is to be completely knowledgeable in the range of pricing of the furniture you'll be suggesting for every room you will be working on with your customers.

I call this process your floor inventory audit.

## Your Auditing Method

You can work alone or with a group on this project. Groups usually become more involved and more information is uncovered as people ask different questions. Group auditing is faster than individual work, but the work has to be done either way if you are to truly accomplish your first goal: to know everything about what is physically in your store.

Start by reviewing your vendor information and knowing where all the vendor catalogs and price lists (if your store uses them) are stored. Do not, however, bring any catalogs to the floor.

Work first with the category of upholstered furniture, because this is the biggest overall category of sales, and it is the one with the most options and things to learn. (Don't work by vendor.) Proceed group by group as the groups and items are displayed from your first group. Here's a partial list of the knowledge you are seeking about each product:

- » What is the price point of the sofa and each other upholstered item?
- » What is the shown fabric and its fiber content and price level?
- » Is this a special order group or only available as shown (you'll need catalog time for this work)?
- » Is there a "value pack" selection of other fabrics at the same price?
- » What other items are available in this style group?
- » What are the fabric choices?
- » How do you price and write special orders?
- » What is the turn-around time for special orders?
- » What items are in stock for quick delivery to customers?

» What are the construction methods for frames, springs, cushions, etc.?

» What is the quality of leather covers? Top grain, splits, enhanced, corrected, etc.

» Is the item all leather or a leather/vinyl combination?

The above are some of the factual things you need to know, but there are some subjective things such as comfort, firmness of seating, depth of seat, and others that you should pay attention to for advising and guiding customers. You need to sit in every piece of upholstered furniture.

As you work on the floor, write your questions down on an ongoing list. At the end of your sessions, your manager or trainer will respond to all your questions to which you can't otherwise find answers. I suggest that you work a few hours on the audit, then go to your catalogs and find all the groups that you've audited in the appropriate vendor catalog and price list. After a few hours you will have several groups for each of your vendors, so one trip to the catalog will help you find the necessary information for them all. Save any questions that you can't answer this way for the later meeting with your manager/trainer or the factory representative.

For most traditional furniture stores, bedrooms are the second-largest selling category, representing around 25 percent of all furniture shopping. The overall category includes most youth furniture as well as adult bedrooms. Auditing this category is easier than the upholstery category, but extremely important. You need to know every option available for beds, because beds sell bedrooms. For many groups you sell there will be as many as four different beds available that you can order from the vendor. This can often be the difference between making and losing a sale, so pay attention to the bedroom category.

For bedrooms and all other wood categories, you have some different things to learn:

- » Finish options
- » The basic wood used in construction of face surfaces
- » The wood used in structural and support pieces
- » The joining techniques, such as dovetailed drawers, mortise, and tenon joining
- » Finishing steps
- » How rails are handled and attached to the headboard and foot board
- » The use of veneers in case piece tops and side panels
- » How table leaves are installed, stored, etc.
- » How all mechanics work, such as hinges, table glides, drawer guides, lift mechanisms, etc.
- » For wall systems, you need to know what kind and size of electronics can be used with each different group
- » How groups are assembled so as to how electronics can be installed
- » For a home office, you'll need to know how computers can be installed, and what bells and whistles are included to make for optimum use

There are thousands of details you have to learn and remember about the products in your store. Working through the audit system I've described above is the best possible way to accomplish this task, because adults learn by doing, by being involved with the subject of their study, by touching, feeling, and using the products they sell.

The process may take as long as five to seven days to complete. That may sound like a lot of time, but this investment is worth it. When you tell a customer that you have some suggestions to fill the need they have described to you, you will be able to have complete confidence that you posses all the knowledge you need to fulfill your promise.

Once you've completed your initial floor audit, you will have interacted with every item on your store's selling floor. As new items and groups arrive on the floor, your learning will be incremental, adding to your store of knowledge about your vendors. New vendors will require training by the factory representatives.

Your merchandise department should provide training on all new products. They'll fit it into your price/quality mix and provide all catalogs, price lists, and ordering instructions.

## Features, Advantages, and Benefits

I want to stress that there are no benefits to any item a customer buys that do not relate to some need the customer has expressed. Benefits are not inherent in the products themselves, but derive from the products' features as they relate to the customer's needs.

The features of a product define the product itself. A feature of a sofa, for example, is that it has seats to sit on. The kind of seat is also a feature. The advantage is that you don't have to stand up or sit on the floor. The benefit might be that you'll be more comfortable and feel better sitting on the sofa. Feeling better is the most pervasive benefit that most customers are looking for; it doesn't matter whether it's feeling better physically or emotionally, as long as it works for your customer.

Features are the things the product has, its attributes. Solid wood is a feature. Veneering is a feature. A 15-step finish is a feature, and a 3-step finish is a feature. Dovetailed drawers are a feature, as are nailed drawers. Different features carry different costs. Solid wood is costlier than some veneers because of the way the raw materials are processed and consumed, but some veneers are applied to solid wood sub-surfaces, making them yet more expensive than even solid wood.

The 15-step finish is more costly to produce than the 3-step finish, but the advantage is that such finishes are deeper, less likely to fade, and wear better than 3-step finishes. The benefit to your customer might be, depending on what they've told you, that their furniture will still look great many years into the future. Another benefit that you should be aware of is that perhaps owning the best is what this particular customer really wants.

Eight-way, hand-tied deck springs have always been the gold standard in upholstery construction. However, there are differences in how this process is executed, just as there are ranges of performance and quality in all areas of life. Eight-way, hand-tied construction is not inherently better than other types such as web, drop-in spring units, or sinuous wire construction. A lot depends on the application; for example, you cannot use eight-way, hand-tied in some styles of non-skirted, off-the-floor, period items or in motion upholstery.

Though it's rare that a customer will ask you about these things, you need to know them so you can explain some of the large differences in price among various groups on your floor. What, for instance, would account for a price difference of $4,000 or more between one five-piece bedroom and another? There can be many reasons for this wide variance, from raw materials' costs, through manufacturing costs, to quality of construction and finishing, to shipping materials and finished products across the world, and to margin needs of your company. However, fundamentally, the way things are made and what they are made of will account for most of the variance. Be prepared to explain these things to your customers when you have to, but don't waste your time or your customer's patience explaining things if they don't want to know.

I believe that these issues are among the reasons customers decide not to buy today. They don't understand these price/quality variances as they browse, and don't know enough about furniture construction and manufacturing to see for themselves. They just get confused, uncertain, and frustrated, and go home.

## Developing Your Store Tour

Now that you've learned about every item in your store, the relative price points by category, and the features and advantages of them, you should take the time to develop a tour you will use to guide customers. This is important to show your customers you are an expert in your field, and to help those customers who are not targeted on any specific look or style.

Every category you studied in training requires a guided tour, and I use that term because it brings to mind a tour guide in a museum who appears to be an expert on what's displayed there. You'll generally be touring only one category or sub-category at a time, and your tour should not take more than a few minutes while you seek feedback from your customers throughout. Just ask them what they think.

You want to show your customers different broad style looks and price points not only to help get their feedback but also to show them options without having them aimlessly wander the store and not really see anything. As an example of how to structure your tour, think of the different styles of full upholstered, non-motion furniture your store carries. There will usually be contemporary looks along with traditional, transitional, and period. If your sofas start at $700 and top out at $1,600, the group pricing will show large dollar variation, and you should show your customers items that your work with them has indicated are right for them.

Then there are leather items to show and present that will demonstrate different price points and ranges of styles and quality. Customers who haven't considered leather furniture before will need a primer on the qualities of leather and what to look for. Make sure you can do it.

Know all of the quality aspects and be able to guide your customer through the maze of options quickly and effectively. Don't waste people's time showing them everything on your floor; they don't need you for that. While customers report liking a big selection, they need you to edit that selection for them, based on what you learn about them and their room.

## Benefit-Driven Product Presentations

Presenting products to your customers means more than just showing and telling, which is how salespeople make presentations when they haven't really connected to their customer's needs. These salespeople ask questions such as:

*"What room is it for?"*

*"Do you have a particular style in mind?"*

*"Do you have a particular color in mind?"*

I call these "dumb" questions for several reasons. First, asking a customer what room the item is for is a question that your customer can answer without offering any important information. "It's for our family room" only begs the next question, which should be "Tell me about the room," but I've heard hundreds of people then ask the "style" and the "color" questions. These are the very things your customer is depending on you to show them. People don't shop for furniture very often — for example, the average consumer keeps their living room sofa for eight years, and some for much longer. They want advice on new styles, new fabrics and colors, and new technologies.

After you've taken your customer through the room analysis process, using a simple room sketch as your tool, you have in your hands a physical representation of their room. You now will use the sketch and all the information you've garnered through the process to make product presentations that address the benefits your customer has told you are important to her.

There are two important ways you'll use your sketch and customer lifestyle information in presenting products to your customers:

1. To connect the product to the room
2. To connect their expressed needs to the features and advantages of the products

Connecting the product to the room is an important psychological connection you want to make. Here's how it should sound: "This reclining chair will look great right here next to the fireplace" (point to the sketch). It's that simple. Making the connection to the room is a simple concept that you cannot use if you don't have a representation of the room.

Remember that your selling strategy makes it clear that you want the customer to come first in everything you do. That makes it important that your product presentations target your customers' needs. Always put the benefit first and the features second.

**The wrong way:**

"This reclining chair has a multi-position footrest that is handle operated, and a backrest that can be positioned anywhere along its arch. It's perfect for watching TV, reading, or just relaxing."

**The right way:**

"This recliner allows you to watch TV, read, or just relax because it has a multi-position, handle operated footrest, and a backrest that can be positioned anywhere along its arch."

The features are only important insofar as they support the benefits that support the customer's needs.

## Handling Customer Feedback

Your customers won't like everything you present. I dislike the term "objections," and I particularly dislike the idea of "overcoming objections." You can't overcome objections; you can just deal with them in a customer-centered way. I call a customer's negative comments about the things you show to be simply feedback — which is exactly what you asked for. Feedback helps you ensure you're on the right track, and if you're off-track, you want to find out early in your engagement, not at the end. You might have missed something. Perhaps you didn't ask all the right questions, or misunderstood an answer. Maybe your customer wasn't clear or used the wrong terminology — there are dozens of things that can go wrong in communications with relative strangers. Feedback from customers, whether positive or negative, is your way of knowing where you are and clarifying your understanding.

Handling them is simple, and you don't have to do any "selling" to do it. Just say thank you.

*"Thanks for telling me that, because it's knowing your feelings and ideas about the things I show you that will help me help you better."*

You always want to welcome and support your customer's feedback regarding the things you show them. You have ample tools at hand to help you deal with most of the things customers are concerned about, and as they give you more feedback, you become more connected to them on a personal basis. Here are the most common aspects about which customers are uncertain, and how you can handle them in this strategic selling system:

» The appearance of the merchandise — the style issue.

   » This is the first thing to deal with, but it's the whole reason you take the approach of telling your customer up front that you are showing them things explicitly to get their feedback on things they like and don't like.

   » You know that many people look at a sofa fabric only, and if they don't like it, they will pass the style completely. This is the most common appearance issue you'll face, and when you stay in control by touring first and then homing in on looks they like, you're ahead of the game.

» The price of the merchandise.

   » This is important to help customers get their spending plan together. Most people don't shop for furniture often; these are durable products that don't wear out quickly. Even though prices of most furniture items have been stable over the past three decades, the growth in the breadth of goods has customer's heads spinning.

   » Most people don't plan a room. They buy one thing at a time and try to build a beautiful room. It seldom works, and the rooms seldom get done, so planning a room and helping them plan their purchases for the room is a value you bring to the relationship. Price feedback is a very good thing.

*"Your feedback is really helpful to me. I feel that part of my job is to help people understand the balance between price and quality, in other words, the value of the things they buy. This kind of feedback helps a lot."*

Don't try to overcome your customer's objections. Join with them to solve their problems, and look at their feedback as them assisting you in helping them get the room and home they want.

## Getting to "Yes"

As you present product solutions to you customers, don't forget that problem-solving is also selling. In selling, you have to reach agreement with your customer that the solutions you present are right for them. It's better to do this along the way than to be surprised when you attempt to close and find out that the customer isn't convinced that your suggested solution is the right one.

As you make suggestions to customers, whether of products or processes, always take time to ask; "Do you agree?" Do this often so you build a foundation of agreement along the way.

- ⇒ "I think this sofa is very comfortable, do you agree?"
- ⇒ "This layout gives you flexibility and addresses your need for everyone to see the TV. Do you agree?"
- ⇒ "This group is well-priced and gives you all the storage you need. Do you agree?"
- ⇒ "Don't you agree that it's important to have plenty of seating around the table?"
- ⇒ "Can we agree that a sofa and loveseat seems to fit better than a sectional?"
- ⇒ "Do you agree that comfort is the most important thing when buying a mattress set?"

There are endless opportunities to do this, but I've found that many salespeople don't take advantage of them. This almost always comes back to haunt you when it's time to close your sale.

In the next chapter you'll learn how to offer total solutions to your customers depending on all the things you've learned about them, their homes, rooms, and dreams for creating beautiful homes.

# CHAPTER 7

## Offering
## Customer-Centered
## Solutions

We developed our selling strategy to address issues that consumer research and our own experience and results show we need to address in order to improve sales. Your selling strategy, and your selling system has brought you to the point where you are ready to offer solutions to your customer based on what you now understand are her broader needs.

## Four Levels of Service

Your strategy team determined that you could capture additional sales by offering more help to those customers who need it, and your salespeople can determine which customers these are by taking all their customers down a defined path based on information about the room they're working on and the nature of their project.

In this Chapter, we'll spell out and define the four levels of service you will offer to ensure that you get every revenue dollar possible out of your customer traffic by elevating the levels of service you provide to all customers. There are no sales tricks in this strategy. There are no "high-impact sale" techniques, no false markups nor other specious tactics that will hurt you in the future, and no gimmicks. These options show how your salespeople may move forward with a customer.

1. Your first level of service is to those customers who don't need any additional help regarding their room design or layout. These customers will purchase to-day if the following things are in place:
   a. A good selection
   b. A great sale event
   c. Long-term financing
   d. Goods in stock for immediate delivery
   e. Salespeople who are nice, competent, polite, and know your merchandise
   f. A product that suits their taste and is in their price comfort zone

   I have always maintained that, even for these "easy" sales, you better serve your customers by dealing with their room. Whether or not you sketch the room depends on the specific situation with each customer, but you can never know when this simple discussion around the question "tell me about your room" will produce some additional need, whether for today or in the future. This is the way you can sell one more item to a customer, like a lamp or a table, an additional nightstand, or an armoire that they didn't think would fit their room.
   I have witnessed the sale of bedroom armoires to customers who wanted to buy one but thought they couldn't fit one in their room. Sketching by the salesperson led to the use of the electronic room planner, which led to a new room layout that al-lowed room for the armoire, a substantial increase to the purchase. People become stuck on the room layout they've always had and can't see the room any other way.

There is no downside to offering more service, more help to your customers, as long as you recognize when its time to close and move on to your next customer.

2. Your next level of service requires that your salespeople understand that the customer they're serving isn't satisfied with the list of good things you showed them in the first level — they need a little more help. For them you need to:
   a. Discuss the room they're working on
   b. Sketch the room and use your room-planning software to do a quick, to-scale room layout on screen

   Only when your customer feels secure that the item will fit the room, both in size and décor, will they purchase

3. The third level of service is for those customers who are working on a bigger project than just the furniture they are shopping for today. This is discovered through the sketching process. It requires more work today, and more involvement by your salesperson and your staff designer. This In-Store Room Planning project will likely result in a purchase of anywhere from 3 to 5 times your store's average sale.
   a. Elicit as much information as you can during this first visit. Get a feel for what the customer likes and dislikes, and try to agree on some major furniture pieces to fit into your room plan for her. Make sure you cover the furnishings budget, and don't let her leave until you have an agreement around the potential sale amount. Then, don't ever exceed it.

    b. Explain the entire process to your customer so they have no fear or doubt about what the process includes.

    c. Make an appointment (a Be-Back) for her to return with the correct room sizes, photographs, color samples, fabrics, and carpet samples — everything you need to put her room together with her. At this time you'll once more review the budget for the project and the furniture selections, and make another appointment for her final presentation.

    d. Your salesperson and designer will work together on putting together the final to-scale floor plan, the fabric selections, and the furniture items that fall within the customer's budget.

This customer will not purchase today, and in fact may not have purchased at all had you not provided this level of service. My experience shows that you can offer this level of service to as many as three percent of your customers. That means that three out of every hundred customers would choose to work with you this way provided there were no additional cost to them. Close rates on such projects should approach 100 percent if you've done everything right.

You'll find a detailed description of the In-Store Room Planning process in the Appendices at the end of this book.

4. The fourth level of service, and the highest you can offer in your business, is the house call. This is a time- and resource-consuming service, and only those customers with the largest projects should qualify. Again, you will discover this during the

"understanding" phase through asking all the right questions and sketching the room. House calls will result in sales that are six to 10 times greater than your store average sale.

a. This level of service requires a lot of work in the store during the first visit. The investment is worth it in the end, but you must be careful to fully explain the entire process and predict what will happen at each phase.

b. You'll make an appointment to visit the customer's home and determine who will attend. Usually, both the salesperson and the designer will cooperate on the house call so both fully understand the customer's situation and needs. This is a one-hour visit.

c. You will also make another appointment at the same time for your customer to return to the store for the final presentation of the completed room. Setting up both appointments at the same time frames the project in the customer's mind and yours. I suggest that you limit all such projects to a 14-day period.

Your sales managers must be able to oversee all of the processes discussed above: In-store sketching and selling today, in-store room-planning projects, and house call projects. You'll make this possible by ensuring that all of the processes are written in the systematic format shown above. Everyone does the same things, follows the same steps, and documents the process in the same way.

Your selling strategy is to offer more help to all customers. This means automatically offering help to the 80 percent of shoppers who don't buy on their first visit to your store (the inverse of your 20 percent average close rate).

## Room Planning Software

Customers love this stuff. Room-planning software — such as the programs available from Icovia®, Micro-D®, and others — is a necessary part of every furniture retailer's strategy. Many retailers and manufacturers have these tools in place on their websites, but the technology needs to be in the store where your salespeople are face-to-face with your customers. If you leave this up to customers to use on your website, you're missing a valuable connection tool you should offer right on the selling floor.

When I hear objections that using the software on the floor takes too much time, I reflect back on the metrics. Eighty percent of customer visits to furniture stores don't result in a sale. Forty percent of shoppers tell us that there are too many options, and they can't relate to the design issues related to their potential purchase. The range of performance of groups of salespeople in close ratio and average sale is as large as 40 percent — the lowest person performs at 60 percent of the rate of the highest person.

Research has shown us that a large majority of our customers need more help, but some retailers feel that it takes too much time on the floor to give it to them. Does this mean that you are willing to let the business go rather than take strategic actions to capture it? This is one of those issues that I encounter in many stores that is so illogical that I can't make any sense of it.

For most retailers, selling just one more out of every ten who shop, would increase their business by 50 percent. I can think of no other action or strategy that will capture that one more customer other than offering more help to those who need it and want it, and the room-planning software in your store is one key element in this strategy. You need to have a computer-based room planner on your website and you need it in a prominent place on your selling floor. Perhaps, depending on your store's layout, you need to have multiple locations where customers and salespeople can access and use the room planner.

I like these room planners, because when you prominently display a room planner on the selling floor, its mere presence makes a powerful statement about the amount of help customers will receive in your store. Every salesperson will be trained and be expert at using the tool. The more they use it, the easier it becomes.

Sometimes, when discussing an item with a customer, the question of fit will be an issue. You know the routine: "we just have to go home and measure to be sure it will fit." This comes up very often with sectional groups, but is a standard fear customers have. Just showing them how you can help them, or how they can help themselves on your company's website can lead to a quality Be-Back, a follow-up call or email, and a sale that you might not otherwise make. That's because this is another example of more help than they're used to getting in retail stores.

In your higher-level services, Room Planning and House Calls, the computerized room planners allow for very professional presentations from salespeople who are not professional designers.

Many manufacturers offer a Room Planning tool on their websites. If you work with any of these manufacturers, you can link your website to their room planner (with permission) and save the cost of having your own. The drawback to doing this, however, is that you don't capture customer information as you would if the tool resided on your company site, and your company logo doesn't print on Room Planners. I think these are major drawbacks to using manufacturer room planners.

I believe that the tool is so important in today's marketplace that you should do all you can to have one with your logo on your website. The large regional retailers I know who have a Room Planning tool on their websites have also invested heavily online cataloging. There is no need to do this, because all of the room planners I'm familiar with also offer generic icons that you can resize on the spot to represent any products you carry.

In Chapter 8 you'll see how all you've learned so far is brought together in a natural way so that closing isn't really a separate step at all.

# CLOSING YOUR SALE

**Our Mission**

*It is our mission to serve our community by helping our customers understand how to use our home furnishings products to enhance the beauty and comfort of their homes and the quality of their lives. We will always provide fair value to our customers, and will represent our suppliers with honor and integrity at all times. We will strive to provide a high-quality workplace where our employees can prosper and achieve their quality-of-life goals.*

Closing your sale should be a natural outcome of the processes you use to deal with your customers. From the outset of every engagement between a shopper and a salesperson, all parties know that it is your job to close the sale. My position in this regard has always been that, while it's true that closing is your job and your goal, it cannot be your first job. Your first jobs are to serve, to understand, and to offer solutions, then to close.

My take on closing is that I don't believe salespeople lose as many sales due to not having good closing skills as they lose because of not having good opening skills.

When you try to close sales with shoppers who are not ready to buy, you create a relationship of distrust and fear in the minds of these shoppers. At the same time, if you don't attempt to close with those shoppers who will buy on their first visit, you risk losing sales you should have made.

## Closing First-Time Shoppers Today

You've greeted your customer with a smile and a welcoming word. You've listened to their request and know not only what they're looking for but also what they're trying to accomplish for themselves, their room, and their quality of life.

They like what you've shown them and the price is within their comfort range. You have the products in stock or can get them within their required timing. So, close the sale. Just say:

*"This sofa seems to be just what you're looking for. The look is what you want, it's comfortable for everyone, the price is great, and we can have it delivered on Friday. You've made a great choice. You're going to love this piece in your room."*

*"Let's write it up."*

It really is that simple, but I've witnessed hundreds of situations where salespeople don't take this simple step to close. Many have told me they believe that this is "pushy"; they want the customer to say, "Oh, we love it, please write it up!" I have even heard a salesperson suggest that a customer "go home and think about it." The thinking seems to be: I did my part, now it's up to my customer to buy.

Selling doesn't work that way. Selling requires assertiveness along with problem-solving, presentation skills, and the understanding that you cannot help a shopper enhance their quality of life unless you turn them into a customer. You can't fulfill your mission until people buy. If you've done your job, your customer now views you as a knowledgeable, caring professional. The need you to tell them that it's OK to buy, that it's the right thing for them, and that they've made a great decision.

## Nothing Fails Like Success

Some closes with those easy-to-sell customers will be almost automatic, and the danger for non-assertive salespeople is that their success with these easy-to-sell customers causes them to believe that this is the right way to sell. In other words, nothing fails like success. When poor selling behaviors still result in sales, there is a reinforcement of those poor behaviors, so people keep doing those things. In my opinion, this breeds mediocrity and keeps salespeople and stores from achieving their maximum potential for sales and income.

## Closing the Harder-to-Sell Customer

A higher percentage of customers are hard-to-sell than are easy-to-sell. This is why closing rates for traditional stores don't usually exceed 20 percent to 30 percent of all customer visits. This means to me, that 70 percent to 80 percent of all the work performed by retail salespeople is uncompensated time. Some customers need more help deciding to make the purchase, even after you've given them more help making their furniture selection.

## Sketching and Room Plans in the Closing Process

Let's look at the steps we've laid out for the selling process to ensure you have connected to your customers on both professional and emotional levels, placing their needs for their rooms at the center of your engagement:

» You've discussed their need and produced a room sketch to help you understand.

» You've taken this a step further for some customers and developed a computer room plan to ensure proper scale and layout.

» You've used this information to present some product solutions that meet their needs.

» You've dealt with customer feedback on these products, and arrived at a solution they like.

» For special orders, you've spelled out the wait time,
   and have agreed you can have in their home when
   they want it.

When you've done all this, you've provided your customer with the "more help" they need. Your first step is to
quickly, but thoroughly review all the areas of agreement.

*"This group is just what you're looking for. The
look is what you want, it's comfortable for everyone, the price is great, and we can have it
delivered when you need it. You've made a great
choice. You're going to love this room."*

*"Let's get your order placed."*

# CHAPTER 9

# MAINTAINING LONG-TERM CUSTOMER RELATIONSHIPS

Almost all retailers I have engaged with over the years have commented on, or complained about, the lack of customer loyalty they witness in their businesses.

The thing that many retailers don't seem to understand about customer loyalty is that you have to earn it. In building and developing stores that sell things as personal and important to quality of life as the furniture people choose to surround themselves with and live with every day, there is high value placed by relational consumers on the quality of the shopping experience. Because we know that people aren't always either transactional or relational, there is reason to believe that at least some transactional shoppers will act more relational when buying home furnishings.

## Developing Your Customer Base

The salespeople I've worked with over my career have one common weakness that causes them to perform at far lower levels than they could. They don't understand about building a broad base of satisfied customers and keeping them in their sphere of influence through constant contact.

In many other businesses — insurance, financial instruments, and real estate come quickly to mind — professional salespeople live on their customer base for repeat business and referrals. Smart retail salespeople don't want to have to depend for their livelihood on the next customer to come through the door. Yet this is not the case in the furniture business, and it's one more reason that stores and salespeople have consistently underperformed.

This is not to say that no one does it; I know of two such individuals who earn mid six-figure annual income and take no new customers. They live off their past customers and their referrals, and their referrals' referrals. The important thing to understand is that it's not difficult to do. It's all in the way you think about your life and your work.

Using the figures I laid out in Chapter 2 on metrics, full-time furniture salespeople would engage with 1,560 customer opportunities each year. Given that around 15 percent of them are Be-Backs (customers who return on the same project) that means that salespeople will see 1,326 new customers per year. This means that a 5-year veteran will have engaged new 6,630 customers in those years. With a 25 percent close ratio, they will have closed 1,658 sales. Given that people buy furniture seldom, but do have many different rooms to work on, those 1,658 buyers equal more than one year's worth of customers at the door.

The people who have bought from you are the first, best resource for future business, particularly the relational buyers. Again, if you've served them well, truly connected to their home design desires, and helped them purchase things with the goal of enhancing their quality of life, these thousands of past customers represent a gold mine for you. Think of the reasons why:

❧ They already have invested time and information in their relationship with you.

» They have already had a satisfactory experience with you, and may even have referred other people to you.

» They trust you, and this is what your relational shoppers are looking for.

» They believe you can help them make their next project easier to complete.

» They are pre-disposed to buy from you.

I call these customers "personal trade" customers. They ask for you when they come through the door. Close ratios for personal trade customers are over 50 percent, and when you work to bring them back, you can drive your overall close ratio toward that 30 percent level where the winners are.

The remaining 4,972 shoppers who didn't buy, but shopped, represent over five years worth of new customers. One problem is that salespeople give up completely on the customers who don't buy even though, if they do their jobs as defined in the previous sections of this book, they have a lot of information about those customers, their rooms, and their needs. These are thousands of potential customers. Why just give up on them?

If you engage customers in the way I've described, a relationship exists based around customer issues. You've taken a real interest in them and their home and offered solutions to problems the customer won't easily find elsewhere. Yet, as we know from our research, many customers just can't make the final decision or, in the case of transactional shoppers, won't make it. Your selling strategy will reduce that number for your store, but we have targeted only one more customer out of the ten who don't buy the first time. There are hundreds more who are part of that 40 percent that don't buy early in their quest. Giving up after investing time and work in them just doesn't make sense.

You have to stay connected in the right ways, and you have to have your customer's permission to do so, but customers who know you and return to you on new projects are far more likely to purchase from you than are brand new customers. If you've done your job right, and dealt with their room issues, served them at a higher level than your competitors, you will build a solid base for income into the future.

## Earn the Right to Stay Connected

The first priority for every salesperson is to make the sale today. Historical data show, however, that in more cases than not, this does not happen. The second priority, then, is to develop return shoppers — people who return to you on the same project. Second visits are nearly four times more productive than first visits. Whenever possible, you want to work by appointment with these Be-Back shoppers, and to achieve that goal you have to earn the right to make an appointment for them to return. In other words, they have to value your efforts and their relationship with you. They have to believe you have solutions for their home furnishings needs.

It doesn't matter whether you make the return appointment at the time of the first engagement or as the result of a follow-up contact. What matters is that if you don't make it in the store the first time, you have reason and permission to follow up.

When you use the Room Design Profile form, you begin the process of maintaining your customer base and developing return customers. The profile is a good way to record all the things you talk about with a customer, but nothing is more important than having their contact information. You'll want address, phone, and — more important than ever — e-mail addresses.

To have customers gladly give you all this information requires that you do some things to earn their trust, and that you ask for and receive permission to follow up and contact them in the future. Most salespeople and managers don't always understand the importance of actually asking for permission instead of assuming it.

So, how do you earn the right to stay connected to buyers and non-buyers?

» Greet them gladly with a sincere smile.
» Engage them by concentrating all dialog around them and their issues.
» Build trust that you are not just trying to sell them something — that it's not all about you.
» Deal with their real problems and concerns around their room, their homes, and their quality of life.
» Sketch the room, create an electronic room plan, make their experience one they'll remember.
» Make friends, not just customers, be an advisor. Everyone wants a friend in the business.
» Present solutions they can live with, and help them to buy, today or in the future, because that's how you improve their quality of life.
» Do all these things regardless of whether you think you're dealing with a relational or transactional type of shopper.

Earn the right to say this to every unsold customer:

*"I know you agree that we accomplished a lot today. I have some work to do for you in finding the right (things) and preparing the floor plan. Why don't we make an appointment for you to come back, and I'll have everything ready when you arrive?"*

Earn the right to say this to customers who buy from you:

*"I like to stay in touch with all my customers. If it's OK with you, I'll call you right after your*

*furniture is delivered to see how everything looks and make sure you're happy. May I follow up with you from time to time with special offers and sale reminders?"*

If you've earned the right by doing all the things in your selling system, you'll have no problem getting permission, and you'll develop many more return customers.

## Using E-mail

E-mail is, in my opinion, the best communication method for ongoing, general follow up. You can set up customer groups and easily communicate sale reminders and special offers to large numbers of customers. You can also send personal messages the same way. E-mail is less intrusive than phone calls and messages left on answering machines, and recipients can choose not to open your message.

More retailers are gathering e-mail addresses of shoppers and customers for use in marketing campaigns. E-Marketing is the next big thing in retail home furnishings. Do not assume, however, that your customers are OK with your use of their e-mail for your personal contacts.

For those customers who don't have e-mail, you can still use phone and snail-mail to reach them, but no matter what the method, be sure you get permission.

## Using CRM Software

If your company has any Customer Relationship Management software, make sure you use it. Any CRM program does what you need. Some of the common programs are Outlook, Act, Clientele, and Goldmine. For furniture-specific programs, I recommend Trax® to retailers who have no traffic monitoring or opportunity recording/CRM system available from their operating system supplier. PROFITsystems®, a widely used business operating system for home furnishings retailers, offers the Customer Care Center for this purpose as part of its operating system at no extra charge to clients, and other furniture-oriented systems may offer versions of CRM systems as well.

## The Work of Salespeople

There are five things I believe salespeople should be doing during their time at work in retail home furnishings stores. They are:

1. Working face-to-face with a customer
2. Working on a customer-related project
3. Performing follow up on customer orders
4. Performing follow up communications with customers
5. Working on improving their skills, knowledge, and performance metrics

The complete job description for salespeople is spelled out in Part Two of this book. A lot is expected of you, and you will be compensated at the highest possible level if you apply all the things I've discussed so far. For commissioned salespeople, it's entirely up to you, the way you work, and the things you do. I've laid out a detailed plan for working with customers and doing those things that will improve you sales and your income.

As we saw before, the sales equation in this, and all retail businesses, is:

> **Sales = Customer Opportunities x
> Close Ratio x Average Sale**

Everything developed and detailed regarding this strategy is targeted at improving one or more of the three critical factors. Salespeople now have many different action items to employ to maximize personal sales and income.

Here's how you can improve each of the three critical factors:

### Customer Opportunities

» You improve the quality of your customer opportunities by bringing current shoppers back to you a second time (Be-Backs). Your close ratio for these customers will be over 70 percent.

» Request referrals from customers who you've impressed with your service and friendly, consultative approach to their home design issues.

### Close Ratio

» You improve your close ratio through Be-Backs. Aim for a return customer ratio of 20 percent of your monthly opportunities.

» Provide more help to all customers. Sketch more customers' rooms to connect to their projects. The more you sketch rooms and/or make electronic room plans, the more people will buy from you today and in the future.

» Seek and find that small percent of your total opportunities who want much more service in the form of Room Planning and House Calls. These selling strategies generate automatic Be-Backs, and close rates on these kinds of projects are near 100 percent.

» Continuous customer contact for past and present customers will bring more old customers back to you to buy again on a new project.

### Average Sale

» Sketching and room plans cause some customers to buy more than they originally were shopping for. You improve your Average Sale by providing room-based solutions to your customers' decorating problems.

- » Room planning produces sales that are three to five times higher than your store average.
- » House calls produce sales that are six to 10 times higher than your store average.

## Summary

The selling system has now been developed and documented above. We learned that many customers need more help than we typically offer, that dealing with their room issues and providing very high levels of service around those issues, as well as Room Planning and House Calls, will help us get one more customer out of ten to buy, raising our sales on equivalent customer traffic. It will usually take more than one visit to our store to make these sales, so we've developed a system to ensure that they do come back — a function that is inherent in both of our room design services.

We've added a room planning software package to our website and our stores, and we've put a Customer Relationship Management and performance tracking system in place to aid salespeople and managers perform and monitor selling activity.

Our sales strategy is completely aligned with the goals we established during our strategy development and planning sessions. Now, there's one additional aspect that has to be in place if you're going to succeed. Execution is the job of your store sales managers, and that is our subject in Part Three.

# PART THREE

## *The Sales Management System*

# Introduction to Part Three

## Recap

You've now used consumer research that is specific to our industry to develop a customer-focused selling system that accounts for those critical issues that home furnishings consumers have reported affect their purchase decisions. You've clearly defined your customer engagement strategy that is aimed at improving all three factors in the selling success equation: Sales = Opportunities x Close Ratio x Average Sale.

Your final steps in the strategic planning process are to define the role of sales managers and to put in place your execution plan for this entire strategic initiative. Sales management is the business aspect that will implement all your strategic sales initiatives. The success of your strategy depends on them more than any other segment of your organization, and how they perform will be the single most important influence on what happens. Everything swings on the skill, motivations, and abilities of front-line sales managers. These people lead the people who interact with your customers, and no group of managers holds more influence over how things go at the point of contact than they do.

I believe strongly that sales management in a one-to-one, personal-selling environment means *performance* management, and anything that isn't directly related to sales performance improvement should be taken off these managers' plates. Sales management is not sales administration, or sales order administration, delivery scheduling, customer service, or anything else related to the administering of sales *after* the salespeople successfully write them.

The deadly mistake that most home furnishings retailers make is making their sales manager an administrator instead of a performance coach. I compare this to having the head coach of a professional football team see to the restocking of the hot dog stands during the game! Even with seasoned professional players who are the best in the world at what they do, no professional team could survive even one quarter of a game without a coach in charge.

Many furniture retailers appear to believe that their salespeople are world-class performers who need no coaching, oversight, or leadership during the performance of their jobs engaging customers. How do I know this? Because they leave them alone every day to engage customers with no on-the-floor (field) involvement by managers at all.

To compound this mistake, some operating and sales-order entry systems could be considered to be in the category of Sales Prevention Systems. Computer systems' purpose should be to be the vehicle to enter and track sales so that the systems run the business, and people run the systems. I find often that the actual case is that the people do their jobs, and the system runs the people.

I'm officially introducing the idea of the Sales Prevention System and the Sales Prevention Team to this book so you can decide as you read whether you or your systems should be candidates for either of those designations. Of course, you don't want them to be.

Sales management in retail home furnishings stores is sales performance management, period. Do I mean that sales administration is not important? Of course not. I do mean that the people who perform those support functions are staff people who work in support of salespeople. In retail stores where personal selling is the backbone of the business, either you're in sales, or you're in support of sales. There are no other job classifications, in my opinion.

The art and skill of leading and managing retail salespeople is the topic of Part Three. I've divided the sales management system into a sequence of five parts: a cycle of planning, goal setting, preparation, execution and monitoring of the company's strategic sales plan.

Sales managers need to believe and keep always at the front of their minds that they do not manage teams. They do not lead groups or staffs of people. People do not need to be "managed"; people need to manage themselves. A sales manager's job is to lead and coach individuals, and leadership means that people happily follow this lead. Leadership also means that maintaining a work environment where people have everything they need to perform their jobs well and are able to achieve their personal goals for income, job satisfaction, and personal growth.

Coaching is the art and skill of, first, understanding people as individuals, and second, understanding each person's individual needs and goals. I believe there is not one best way to lead and coach everyone. People have to mentally "hire" you as their coach, and that relationship is private between you and each individual. I have found that people who think they manage groups or teams always fail to effectively lead a great majority of the people. Don't try to manage people. They usually resent it because management feels a lot like manipulation. Find out where they want to go, and lead them to that place.

# CHAPTER 10

## STAFFING YOUR STORE FOR SUCCESS

## Introduction

Your selling strategy indicates that your optimum salesperson staffing model is 130 customer opportunities per month per salesperson. This number provides the highest Revenue-per-Opportunity, your financial guideline to salesperson and sales department effectiveness. Optimum staffing is your number one priority initiative.

There is nothing you can do that will serve you better than to have the right number of salespeople on staff to meet the demands of your store traffic. Nothing you can do in advertising or promotion will produce higher levels of sales improvement than proper staffing and training. In fact, you don't want to put more shoppers into your store if your salespeople can't serve them, because when customers leave after receiving no service and touring your store by themselves, they see nothing but the one common feature of every item on your floor — the price tag.

You exacerbate this in stores that are grossly understaffed, based on measured traffic, by the fact that around 55 percent of your weekly traffic (or more) arrives in your store on weekends. If your store is understaffed for weekends, and nearly every store I've encountered is, your lost opportunity sales are tremendous and calculable when you have an electronic traffic counting system in place.

## The Work of Salespeople

As covered in Chapter 9, I believe salespeople should be doing five things during their time at work in retail home furnishings stores. They are:

1. Working face-to-face with a customer
2. Working on a customer-related project
3. Performing follow up on customer orders
4. Performing follow up communications with customers
5. Working on improving their skills, knowledge and performance metrics

Remember, that the first goal is to make a sale today. If a salesperson doesn't achieve that goal, the next priority is to develop return customers by working in a specified way and obtaining all relevant customer information and following up to bring them back. The third priority is to develop room planning customer projects with those customers who value, deserve, and require that level of help

## Staff for Weekends

There's no way around the simple fact that in order to provide the right level of service to weekend customers, you need to have sufficient staff on site. You cannot make up for it by overstaffing on weekdays. Weekend shoppers are different from weekday shoppers in that there are usually couples shopping together on weekends. This is your salespersons' opportunity to connect with both decision-makers, eliminating the "returning spouse" excuse and providing the opportunity to better understand and impress both parties.

Attempting to serve two separate customer opportunities at once is virtually impossible if you perform your job as defined in Part Two. There are those situations and retail environments where "two-timing" is the strategy. These stores make many sales, and walk away from many sales because of their low level of service to those shoppers who need more help. I argue that fast-track, high-traffic stores also underperform because I know the nature of the purchase decisions customers make. The problem is that these stores make enough sales and profits working this way that they can ignore the lost opportunities. Most independent stores don't have that luxury.

Smart salespeople and sales managers develop a strategy for handling weekend shoppers that intelligently uses the same selling strategy as I've laid out. They realize that close rates on first-time shoppers are going to be minimal, so their personal strategy is to lock up Be-Backs with appointments and room-planning projects and send them on their way so they can lock up another Be-Back appointment or room-planning project. They make Be-Back appointments for weekdays or evenings if they can, and they can do this because they have both parties with them on weekends.

If it is necessary to work with a Be-Back customer on a weekend day, you have to be completely prepared, have potential sales pre-written using worksheets. You must work by appointment, and you must work fast without shorting your customer of attention. You also need to remove yourself from the rotation system or extract yourself from a customer engagement prior to your appointment arriving in the store.

I suggest that measuring monthly traffic counts over a running 90-day period to average out seasonal and short-term influences such as holidays and special events. At the end of each month, drop off the earliest month's figures and maintain a trend line to show whether traffic is increasing or decreasing. Pay particular attention to weekend days over this period, because they will be your staffing guide. If the three-month average Saturday traffic shows that you need 15 salespeople to handle the traffic, staff to that level. The same goes for Sundays, when the traffic flow is condensed into a shorter time. If you don't see a variance between the two days in staffing needs, staff both weekend days equally. I have tracked individual performance for years, and believe that on weekends, a salesperson engages an average of one customer per hour, for eight customers in an eight-hour shift. I also know that the flow of traffic is not evenly distributed. Traffic is heaviest between 11:00 a.m. and 4:00 p.m., but you can only adjust coverage for full shifts, so staff lighter in the early morning hours and the late evening hours. Try overlapping coverage as much as possible during peak traffic hours, starting some late shifts at 11:00 a.m., some at 12:00 noon, and some at 1:00 p.m.

The point of this is that you can do all this because you electronically count traffic, by hourly segment, using one-way counters (in, but not out) and photograph all traffic into (but not out of) the front door. The photos are part of your store's security system, so the cost is a double-duty expense.

In situations where client stores have not electronically counted their door traffic but used a manual system of salespeople logging their customer opportunities, I have found variances of as high as 50 percent when using an electronic system when both systems were operated concurrently. No one was cheating, and no one was lying. They just missed logging that many customers. There is no accurate way to know how many of those missed were engaged by someone and not logged, and how many were not attended to at all.

You must electronically count your traffic. If you don't, you can never know the level of salesperson staffing that is right for your store. You cannot schedule correctly when you do it by "feel" — "I feel we need more coverage on Monday evenings" is not as good as "My traffic system tells me I need more coverage on Monday evenings." Manual counts by receptionists are a little better than salesperson rotation logs, but not much. Customer traffic is the first element in the sales success equation. Everything begins with customers coming through your doors. Don't undervalue the importance.

## Developing Your Staffing Model

My staffing model is 130 customer opportunities per salesperson per month as discussed previously. Yours may be different, but to know what it is you have to have accurate customer counts. In a selling environment where individuals serve customers on-to-one and no sales are made except through salespeople, you have no choice but to know the relative effectiveness of your individual people.

Whatever number of customer opportunities is the 90-day average for your most effective salespeople, those with the highest Revenue per Opportunity, use that number as your staffing model. No guessing, no opinions; just measure everything and follow the numbers.

## Recruiting, Interviewing, and Hiring

Hiring the right people is a difficult endeavor at best; it's an ongoing task that requires time and energy that you could better use in coaching your existing salespeople to higher levels of performance. There will always be employee turnover, but one of your prime goals as a sales manager must be to retain good performing people so your recruiting efforts aren't required too often. You'll learn this in the coaching section below.

You have to be prepared to turn loose your lowest performing people after providing all the training, coaching, and opportunities to succeed that you can. Consultative selling isn't right for everyone. In fact, it isn't right for many people, but the problem for you — the person accountable for generating maximum sales revenue — is that you provide everyone with an equal number of customer opportunities. However, you do not get back an equal number of sales dollars from them all. In fact, your worst performers always get more customer opportunities than your best performers. The reason is obvious: your best people spend more time with their customers doing the right things than do your worst performers.

Recruiting is a far more complex issue than it used to be with the web-based job listing services such as Career Builders, Monster, Craig's List, and others. More complexity than just running one newspaper ad. You will also be much more effective using these tools because you can search for resumes as well as field responses to your job postings. Even when your staff is at full strength, you should spend an hour or two each week searching for good candidates.

Use a testing service for every candidate. I use *Salestestonline*®. They will work with you to make the test meet your specific job requirements, and I find them to be right on in their evaluations. The service is available for nearly every job classification in your company, so check it out. Testing provides a standard platform from which to judge a candidate.

Most testing services provide you with great information about your candidates prior to your interview, giving you a heads-up on potential issues you need to deal with — both in the interview and after hiring. You'll pay per test and there may be a small set-up charge with some services, but I find it to be the most helpful recruiting and hiring tool I've ever used.

### Job Descriptions

Based on your selling strategy, write a formal job description for each position. For salespeople who interact with consumers and are accountable for executing your selling strategy and working with your selling systems, the descriptions are the same for everyone. If you have different classifications of salespeople, such as senior sales consultant or senior design consultant, be sure to spell out the differences.

Here are some things to include in every job description:

» The overall statement of purpose — why the job exists, where it fits in the overall strategy, how it affects corporate results.

» The goals for the job — for sales, be specific around numeric goals. In our ongoing example, we want to see close ratio at 30 percent and average sale at $1,365.

» A complete list of tasks that are included in the job. You'll need a task title and description of each task that is also important for the next item.

» A description of how you and the employee will know when the tasks are performed satisfactorily. I use a three-point measurement system: Below standard, at standard, above standard.

» Scheduling requirements must be included. If weekends and holidays are required, spell it out here in detail.

» Compensation type and range for the job, and methods of earning any applicable bonuses.

There's a sample of a salesperson's job description in the Appendices. Use it as your guide.

### Ideas about Recruiting

» Don't try to hire great salespeople. Make them great.

» Look for intelligence, communications skills, professional appearance, good interviewing skills.

» Have a new hire training program in place.

» Employ the services of a good testing service like *Salestestonline*.

- » Administer the test before your interview. Testing services provide you with valuable interview information.
- Be aware that people you want are working somewhere else.
- When recruiting experienced people, understand all the reasons they want to come to work for you.
- Have new hires reveal their earnings record over last three years.
  - » Be "Reagan-like" — trust but verify.
  - » Contact all previous employers.
  - » Use state police public information for background checks, or use a background checking service.
- Employ a professional drug-testing service.
  - » Applicants must test within 24 hours of your interview. Give no notice; you don't want them to be able to "study" for this test.
- Look for people in other businesses who serve you well, such as restaurants, clothing stores, shoe stores, auto dealerships, etc.
- Don't wait until the last minute to begin your search.
  - » Make this an ongoing initiative.
  - » Reward employees who bring qualified people.
  - » Continuously build a file of available people.
    - ▸ You need as many as 20 applicants to make one hire.
  - » Stay in contact with all good prospects monthly.
- Recruit in the store — put out large signs — don't hide it.
- Use your reader sign if you have one.
- If you use Internet job listing services or classified ads, spell out the two most important details:
  - » Full commission, if this is how you pay.
  - » Weekend and holiday requirements.

- ❧ When ready to hire, make your selection quickly.
  - » Don't make good candidates wait for a decision — you'll lose them.
  - » Notify all current active candidates about your decision.
- ❧ Never settle for a candidate because he or she is the only candidate.
  - » Delay hiring until you have more people to choose from
  - » The cost of training is too high to take chances.
  - » If you have only one or two candidates, increase your recruiting efforts

## Interviewing Tips

Informal interviews are better than formal ones. You'll learn more by having a stress-free conversation with a person than by attempting to observe how they respond to stressful situations. People will open up more to you when your approach to them is friendly and welcoming. If you have a pre-test, as I suggest you do, you can observe behavior against the background of the test results.

I always ask applicants this opening question: "Why are you here today?" Then, just as with customers, I let them talk. I do not interrupt or clarify my question. I then ask 'What do you know about our company?" This will tell me whether the candidate looked online to find information about us, or has any information at all. I'm usually not impressed by people who do no pre-interview investigation of our company. My final opening question is, "Tell me what you think this job is all about." I listen very carefully to their response without interruption.

I'll give the candidate an overview of our company and of the position and ask if they still want to continue. Remember that at this point our pre-screen interview will have culled out all those who do not fully understand the unique demands of retailing in terms of schedules, commission payment plans, and the concept of accountability for performance. I'll ask them now what their earnings goal is for the next 12 months. I'll ask now about past earnings, last year and the past five years. I want to know the most they ever earned in one year — and the least.

I will tell the candidate that I have the results of their sales test, and give them an overview of the key results, but I do this in a friendly way, not to intimidate. I ask the candidate to comment on the overall evaluations of their key personality characteristics. You'll be surprised at how accurate these tests can be.

I want the candidate to tell me about things they've accomplished in their lives and their work careers. I will ask them to share their experiences around things like handling difficult customers, irate customers, and difficult customer service issues.

A key issue to me is how they deal with their goals. Most people don't have goals because they don't have clear pathways to achieve them. They don't deal with the "what" because they don't understand the "how." When someone who has never earned more than $30,000 says he wants to earn $50,000, I simply ask the "How?" His reply opens very interesting doors for discussion during interviews.

If our interview goes well, I like the person, and they are anxious to come to work, I write a letter of intent with qualifications for them to take with them. All offers should be made by mail or e-mail and are not valid until officially signed and countersigned. I always demand a clear drug test before anyone can begin work, and will arrange for that immediately because they have only 24 hours to take the test. I also demand a clear background check, so I ask specifically about what such a check will show. Background checks take a lot longer, so employment may begin but is contingent on me receiving a clear background test. Anyone who has misrepresented his or her background will be dismissed.

# CHAPTER 11

TRAINING —
TEACHING THE
SELLING STRATEGY
TO SALESPEOPLE

## Introduction

If there is one area where most managers are weak, this is it. There are two types of training: new hire training and on-going training. New hires deserve enough formal training to learn everything they need to learn, and they need a dedicated trainer. This is unlikely to be the case in most small independent stores, but that doesn't change the fact that new hires deserve it. Think about the vast amount of information that has to be learned in three major areas:

1. The company, the people, the systems (both administrative and operational), and all the relevant processes
2. The products and services, and the thousands of details associated with them
3. The company's selling system, the style to use in engaging customers, all

In the Appendices I've laid out a sample, four-week new-hire training plan that I suggest you adapt to your needs. Training is better when you have more than one person at a time to train, but still has to be done if only for one person. Training cannot be the job of the sales manager only. If it is, it won't get done well, and there's a high probability it won't get done at all. Spread the work around among all department heads and other staff members who can teach. Make these teachers part of your feedback system on how your new person is doing and whether they believe he or she is learning what is needed.

Sales managers have to make a commitment to training that goes beyond mere words. They should have weekly training for new products or vendors that come to the floor. If the store is like many I've known, when a new vendor, group or item comes to the floor, unless a salesperson is on duty that day, it could be days before sales personnel stumble onto the new merchandise. Assign a team or individual salesperson or staff member the task of training on new items and coordinating training schedules with vendor representatives.

To see how to carry out new hire product training, see Chapter 6. This self-learning system requires a vendor overview by the sales manager and merchandise manager, and only once-a-day meetings between sales managers and trainees. It gets the job done better than any other method I've used, and salespeople like it because it keeps them active and involved.

## How Adults Learn

The learning process for adults, you'll remember, goes something like this:

- ✤ They receive new information such as dialogs and selling methods like sketching rooms.
- ✤ They watch someone who is good at it; like a trainer or teacher, perform it.
- ✤ They practice the new skill in a controlled environment — they sketch coworkers' rooms just as they would with a customer.

» They perform with a customer, perhaps while being observed by a manager or coworker.

» If they succeed, they continue to perform their new skill under coaching by their manager and others.

» If they fail, they take additional training and practice, and go back at it again.

» They perform again with a customer, and provide feedback to their coach or manager.

» After performing successfully several times, and being coached through the process, they have effectively learned a new skill

Adults have to be involved in the learning process because they believe it is important to them.

## Words Do Not Teach

People will not learn new behaviors as the result of simply talking to them. Learning is the active side of teaching for the student. Learning means that you do something new that you couldn't do before; your behavior changes. That's how you, as a manager, know that a salesperson has learned something new — they do things differently, or they do different things, from before. When you see salespeople exhibiting new behaviors, you know learning has happened.

You do have to put the new information out there for people to hear, read, and understand. You want to know that your salespeople understand the information conceptually, and you can discuss these concepts with them either individually or in groups to come to a mutual understanding and agreement about the concepts. This applies to new ideas and strategies like those you've developed for your company.

## Using Scripted Dialogs

Let's say that most of your salespeople have never sold or performed a room design project with a customer. You want them to sell two new "products," Room Planning that they perform entirely in the store, and Room Planning with an In-Home Visit (house call selling). They have to be able to sell these processes as if they are products, except there is no cost to customers for either of these products. If you want this to happen, here are the training steps you have to take:

» Decide how you want salespeople to present your products — exactly what do you want people to say, and the exact words you want used. In other words, you have to tell your salespeople exactly what to say. As much as you might want to think otherwise, you cannot leave this up to your salespeople to do for themselves. If you do, you'll have as many approaches to selling critical processes as you have salespeople, and your results will vary dramatically.

» Write these dialogs down and make each person learn them by heart. Keep them short and completely directed to the issues. Make each person deliver the dialog to you in a private training meeting.

» Go to the floor with individuals and listen to them deliver these dialogs to customers. (See Chapter 13 for a description of coaching on the floor.)

Use the post-it note process in a group meeting to help you develop your dialogs for this and any other part of your selling system. Involve some salespeople in the process of developing dialogs for those selling issues that are critical to maximizing sales. Some important areas are:

❖ Warranties: If you can get your salespeople to offer warranties to every customer, every time, your warranty sales will increase dramatically. They'll increase more if they do it right. Dialogs are important in this case.

❖ Delivery charges: Selling delivery is more than just selling the fact that a truck and two guys will bring their furniture to their home. There should be much more to this process and to the reasons you charge for it, such as proper handling and transportation, accountability for damages to furniture or homes, and your service guarantee if you have one. Don't lose sales or jeopardize relationships over this sometimes contentious issue.

❖ Product presentations: These sometimes require more in the way of explanation than others. For those that have special features, write dialogs for how they will be presented.

❖ Waiting time: If you're doing a good job with inventory management, wait times on stock merchandise won't be too long, but special orders can be problematic, so prepare everyone to be able to talk to customers about this in a positive way.

The more brief and well-thought-out dialogs you have, the more control you have over the point of contact with your customers, and the more easily you can predict outcomes or make necessary changes to how your store and your products and services are offered to customers.

Salespeople will ask if they can use their "own words" as long as they cover all the key points. This always reminds me of one of the humorist George Carlin's comment on using "your own words": "I don't have any of my own words. I use the same ones everyone else uses." This is dangerous ground because managing everyone's various dialogs is nearly impossible for managers to do. If a person is not performing up to par, you want a standard of performance to go to for train-ing that is. Managing individual dialogs is time consuming for managers because they have to approve all such vari-ances from the standard, so let your salespeople do it their way until they fail to perform, then, bring them back to the standard form.

Your decision will be based on a test that runs for at least 60 days from the day you start using dialogs on the floor. You will measure performance for each salesperson in all of the areas where dialogs are used (Room Planning, House Calls, warranties, etc.)

## Role-Playing

» Complete your dialog and print it on one sheet of paper in a large font size

» Set up a two-person training session. Don't use groups larger than two.

» Have both people (everyone) learn the dialog and be able to repeat it to you alone before the role-play session.

» Prepare the role of the customer. Don't make it dif-ficult, which is why you have to prepare it to be read verbatim. If you leave the customer's role up to the participants, they'll mimic the worst, toughest, most belligerent customers they've ever encoun-tered in an effort to show you how silly your dialogs are. Let's say you're working on the Room Planning dialog. You will want a lead-in statement or request by your customer, such as: "This is a really tough room to work with," or "I just can't make up my mind which way to go," or "I've been shopping ev-erywhere." All these statements — and more — will lead to your Room Planning presentation dialog that begins with "We have a great way to help people like you who have difficult or challenging rooms."

Prepare some follow up questions that a customer might ask after your salesperson concludes her dialog with "Wouldn't that be a great way for us to work together to get your room done?" The answers to these follow-up questions are not scripted, but require the salesperson to think and respond. All you're looking for is the way they handle the dialog.

» One person plays the customer, the other plays the salesperson.

» The first time through, the salesperson reads the dialog from the paper copy.

» Switch roles.

» Second round, they use no paper copy, but you coach the salesperson through the dialog.

» Third round, they do it all from memory.

Once you've taken the time to do this with every staff member, your intent and commitment to the dialogs will be clear to everyone. Spending time on an issue shows what you consider to be important, and the way your products and services are presented is very important.

## Teaching Basic Room-Planning Skills

It seems to me that anyone involved in selling furniture should be able to perform the most basic room-planning skills such as room sketching, measurements, room layouts, color coordination, and style selection. They should also have basic knowledge of fibers and fabrics and be able to discuss these issues with customers. For those people with low drawing skills, learning how to use your computer-based room planning program is a must.

Given all that, I know that one reason salespeople don't use sketching as a tool to help them connect better to customers' needs is that they don't know how to sketch — or believe they don't. So make sure you teach them how to sketch and how to lay out a room, and help them understand that sketching is not room planning, which requires a higher-level skill set.

Because our selling strategy includes a staff designer who acts as a consultant to salespeople and their customers and performs room-design project work, we can expect her to help in this basic training. I do not believe in the use of graph paper for sketching, as you do not want to attempt to sketch to scale early in your customer engagement. If using the grid to help people draw straight lines, however, gridlines are a good help.

Here are some of the things I believe your salespeople need to learn:

» Principles of scale
» How to draw almost page-sized rectangles — most rooms are this shape, and even if some are not, this is the right place to start.
» Accepted architectural symbols for items such as windows, doors and door-swings, entryways, half-walls, electric outlets, lamps, and cable connections, and fireplaces.
» Accepted ways of representing key furniture items.

These are the basics that any salesperson needs to be able to draw an effective sketch of a customer's room. By learning these simple things, salespeople will more easily adapt to using electronic room planners that make the entire process very simple and effective.

An effective way for salespeople to practice this technique is first to have salespeople sketch all of the rooms in their own home and submit them , then, in training, have people sketch another person's room from their verbal description — just as would be done with a customer. This is a good opportunity to have your people begin each such training session role playing with the question, "Tell me about your room."

# LEADERSHIP AND THE POWER OF GOALS

## Introduction

Your company, like all companies, consists of individuals, and you know that each person is unique and different from all others. People work for one primary reason — to earn a living. They expect to be paid fairly for their work. They also want to have a sense of belonging and the knowledge that they are contributing to the company. They want to feel important and know that their company, their customers, and their associates value them.

It's the responsibility of ownership and management to create the kind of work environment where these things can happen, and where people can achieve their personal goals. If you do this, you'll have a happier and more productive workplace, and you'll not have the kind of atmosphere that contributes to the we/they kind of thinking that pervades many businesses. If you're at war with your salespeople, or if you try to simply impose new methods on them, don't expect too much buy-in to the things you want to change. This is why I urge you to have one or more salespeople on your sales strategy development team and to keep them involved through training and implementation of all new selling initiatives.

Goals are as much about salespeople doing better as they are about the company doing better, because your entire business is in their hands. Whether or not you bring in any sales revenue at all is up to these people — entirely.

The most pervasive mistake all of us make when dealing with goals is that we spend time developing them, or, more likely making them up; putting them out there; and then completely ignoring them. The amount of management time spent on salespeople's goals is miniscule in most sales managers' total time allotment. I urge you to not make this critical mistake, and to instead put the achievement of individual salespeople's goals at the center of your management program. This is the missing link in every sales performance improvement initiative I've encountered in small and large companies. When you succeed in aligning your efforts to help your salespeople achieve their goals, they will work with you to achieve your goals. Everything — your goals and your people's goals — revolve around everyone working to help your customers achieve their goals.

## Wishful-Thinking Is Not a Goal

Here's a sad truth: Most people have no goals, and those who do have no organized, structured way to achieve them. Everyone will tell you what he or she wants to earn. Few people will tell you what they are willing to do to earn it. Your job as a manager is to help your employees bring their actions into line with their goals, but you first have to bring their goals into alignment with their wishes, and their wishes into alignment with their actions.

When I have a salesperson who has an annual earnings record of around, say, $30,000, and that person tells me during our goals development coaching session that they want to earn $50,000, my first question is "What's stopping you from earning that now?" Their answers invariably center on influences and causes outside themselves. This is not so much "blaming" outside factors as it is thinking that all influences are out of their control.

The list of explanations I get (they don't consider these as excuses) has changed little over the years. Here are some of my favorites, and my responses to them.

» Customer traffic. Of course, in the vast majority of stores there is not an accurate system for counting the number of individual customer opportunities each person gets. Even when there is a system for counting overall traffic, this data collection is seldom taken to the individual salesperson level. This means that the salesperson's opinion is as valid as management's opinion causing a stalemate in resolving performance problems.

My handling of this thinking is based on detailed electronic monitoring of the number of individual customer opportunities and of total store traffic. I look first at the average number of individual opportunities per salesperson compared to my 130 per-month-per-person average standard to determine whether it meets my target. Some people will be above this level and some below, so I look at the average for all people with similar schedules.

Next, I look at the Revenue per Opportunity by person to see where each individual is on the range of performance. I compare current data to longer-term data that I maintain to see if there are current anomalies such as one extraordinarily large sale that would cause me to have to adjust comparative results. If the person I'm working with on goal development is in the below-average group of performers in RPO, the traffic reason becomes a non-issue in why this person may be under-performing relative to her goals.

The customer opportunity number also helps me deal with the "worst customer" excuse. Salespeople have to be introduced to the world of statistical probability that will show it to be impossible for all the "bad" shoppers to be distributed to one person over the long term.

» Reluctant customers / "I get the worst customers." Customers are a favorite target for low-performing salespeople. When asked about those salespeople who do perform at high levels of sales and income, the reasons become even more absurd. "She gets all the good opportunities," or, more likely, "They steal all my good customers." Of course, low-performing sales people do make some sales, but they make them exclusively to that 20 percent of customers who are "easy to sell." Their "worst" customers are those who need more help than low performers choose to provide, and the syndrome I discussed earlier in this book bolsters their argument: nothing fails like success. Because these low performers succeed some of the time, their methods work enough of the time to keep them doing those same things, and only those things.

My first place to look to overcome this "objection" is at the number of Be-Back customers logged by this person and the percentage of Be-Backs to overall opportunities. I compare this to the entire staff's results because this number tells me how this salesperson is connecting to customers and whether he's doing the right things to get the nonbuyers back. By knowing the number and percentage of Be-Back opportunities, I can calculate this person's first-time shopper and Be-Back close ratios. If these are lower than my historical baseline data for all sales people, I can eliminate the "I get all the bad customers" objection.

The problem for underperforming salespeople always lies in their ability to develop quality Be-Backs from the 80 percent or more of shoppers who don't buy on their first visit to the store. In the retail home furnishings business, you live on Be-Backs.

» Poor merchandise selection. Salespeople are apparently experts on merchandise selection, pricing, and promotions. When looking at sales by salesperson by category however, I usually find huge opportunity for improvement in areas where other, high-performing salespeople show success.

» Competitive reasons abound among salespeople seeking outside excuses for their low performance. This or that company has better prices and promotions, better location, better merchandise selection, better delivery, and so on.

Every salesperson on your staff deals with the same product lineup, prices, promotions, and competition — the best performers, and the worst. Just look at the short and long-term performance in all critical metrics, opportunities, close ratio, average sale, Be-Backs, design project work, and category performance, and you'll be able to counter all excuses.

## Understanding How Sales Metrics Help You

One of the primary benefits of being metrics driven in your management approach is that it removes as much subjectivity and guesswork from goal setting as possible. Goals development means using historic performance data to identify the areas where each person needs to learn new behaviors and take new actions, then writing your goals equation for each of the factors.

Whenever you hear the excuses in the above section, base your responses on your store's performance data, which is where all of the answers to individual performance problems are. Some CRM systems track all the performance data you need to help any salesperson who is willing to change what they do to achieve their goals. The performance data gathered and reported by most of the performance-tracking systems include:

- ❧ Overall store customer traffic counts
- ❧ A record of each customer opportunity for each salesperson
- ❧ A record of the number of sales closed with these opportunities — the close ratio
- ❧ A record of the merchandise value of each sale used to calculate average sale
- ❧ A record of the category or categories each customer was shopping for
- ❧ A place to record and store all customer contact information and notes on each visit
- ❧ A customer follow-up system using calendar prompts
- ❧ A system to record sales goals and daily, weekly, and monthly reports on performance versus goals to keep people on track
- ❧ Daily performance feedback to individual salespeople and managers
- ❧ Comparison reports for managers on current and past months.

I want to highlight some things here that apply to goals management.

1. Be careful about the way you calculate average sale. Remember, average sale and average ticket

are not the same measure. Average sale is the same as average purchase; it reflects, when measured over time, how a salesperson works with their customers. Average ticket merely shows how they write sales orders. Many stores require that certain categories of merchandise be ordered separately from others which would cause average sale and average ticket to be very different.

2. To accurately measure close ratio, you must account for every customer opportunity — and you must have a high level of accuracy and reporting by all salespeople. No one can be allowed to cheat by under-reporting their opportunities, because in goals management, they truly are cheating themselves. All CRM systems I'm familiar with use the opportunity tracking system to manage the salesperson rotation system. Salespeople have to account for every customer they serve in real time in order to take another customer; CRM systems make the information entry simple and fast so the reporting system doesn't interfere with the flow of business.

3. When you have your overall store sales success equation for sales (Sales = Opportunities x Close Ratio x Average Sale), compare individual results to that to determine who needs help and in which area of performance. (See Chapter 9 for explanations of how you can improve each factor.)

4. To help a salesperson develop their goals, you have to provide them with the pathway to them. For people for whom you have at least 90 days' data on performance, you must be able to show them exactly what values they have to achieve for customer

opportunities (130 per month in our strategic plan), close ratio, and average sale, and how to achieve these levels using your selling strategy.

You'll also use the 90-days' data to show the "wishful thinkers" how they have to change their behavior, actions, and thinking to get to that $50,000 earnings goal they set for themselves. Remember that the one factor in the success equation they cannot change is the number of customer opportunities they will get. No one can predict this with accuracy, so you'll use past performance to predict future traffic.

### Adjusting Your Metrics

You know that to achieve your company goals your company's close ratio has to be at 30 percent or higher, and your average sale has to be at $1,500 or higher. You know that the number of Be-Back customers needs to be at 15 percent of total customer opportunities or higher, and that the number of room-planning projects developed each month should be between two and three percent of total customer opportunities in order for.

Let's say that your overall store traffic is trending down due to a broad economic slowdown such as that experienced in 2007-2009. If you choose to make no reductions in staff and your estimated number of opportunities is 20 percent lower than for a similar period last year, you'll be planning on 104 opportunities per month per person. Does this mean that your revenue and the salespeople's income must go down by 20 percent? It does unless you adjust the other factors in the sales equation upward. A 10 percent improvement in your long-term close ratio, and a 13 percent increase in your long-term average sale would make up for a 20 percent drop in customer traffic.

Here's what your sales equation might look like:

Let's say you started with this scenario:

*A. 130 Opportunities x 20 percent Close Ratio x $1,350 Average Sale = $35,100*

Your new scenario will look like this:

*B. 104 Opportunities x 22 percent Close Ratio x $1,526.50 Average Sale = $35,109*

## Dealing with the Wishful-Thinker

We need to look at how you will handle the $50,000 (income) wishful-thinker's goal development. Let's say you are working with an individual who performs at the level shown in example A above. This person will sell a total of $421,120 over 12 months, and at six percent commission, his earnings will be $25,272 for the 12 months. How can he get to double that amount without changing the number of customer opportunities?

Let's suppose his close ratio could move to 30 percent and his average sale to $1,780. His equation will then be:

130 Opportunities x 30 percent = 39 sales @ $1,780 = $69,420. Annualized, this would be $833,304, and at 6 percent commission, he'll earn $49,982.

This is one way to use sales metrics, both for the long and short terms, to lay out directions to goals for salespeople. Next you have to lay out the actual roadmaps, showing them how they will apply each strategic initiative in your customer engagement strategy to achieve the necessary improvements (see Chapter 8, which spells out the connections between strategic initiatives and salesperson actions). These connections define the road map you have to create for each person.

Here's how you can improve each of the three critical factors in the sales success equation:

### Customer Opportunities

» You improve the quality of your customer opportunities by bringing current shoppers back to you a second time (Be-Backs). Your close ratio for these customers will likely be over 70 percent.

» Referrals you request from customers who you've impressed with your service and friendly, consultative approach to their room design issues.

### Close Ratio

» You improve your close ratio through Be-Backs. Aim for a return customer ratio of 20 percent of you monthly opportunities

» Provide more help to all customers. Sketch more customers' rooms to connect to their projects. The more you sketch rooms and/or make electronic room plans, the more people will buy from you today — and in the future.

» Seek and find that small percentage of your total opportunities who want much more service in the form of Room Planning and House Calls. These selling strategies generate automatic Be-Backs, and close ratios on these kinds of projects are near 100 percent.

» Continuous customer contact for past and present customers will bring more old customers back to you to buy again on a new project.

### Average Sale

» Sketching and room plans cause some customers to buy more than they originally were shopping for, helping you to optimize each sale. You improve your Average Sale by providing room-based solutions to your customers decorating problems.

» Room Planning produces sales that are three to five times higher than your store average

» House Calls produce sales that are six to 10 times higher than your store average

## Goals Drive Performance

Goals should drive performance, but my experience is that they don't. The whole idea of goals, meaningful goals, leaves most people rolling their eyes. Their lack of trust that they can achieve much more for themselves is always reflected against the reality they have lived. They have also never been involved in the processes described here. A further problem lies in the way people view their reality, believing that they're destined to achieve little. Interestingly, people who believe they are not limited by their past experiences do a lot better, sometimes a whole lot better. I believe that if you believe it will happen, then it will: You are the creator of your experiences.

Whether goals drive performance is determined more by what managers do than by what salespeople do. Long ago, when I first began to work with goals as a sales manager, I learned the one most important thing a sales manager must do to make goals drive performance is to put them at the front of everyone's mind and keep them there. In the beginning, I felt that I cared more about their goals than they did.

Salespeople deal with two kinds of goals: Their own and the ones you set for them. If your goal-setting is purely top-down, as it would be with a "fair-share" environment where the store financial goal is divided equally among the salespeople based on scheduled hours, don't expect too much buy-in from your people. Our entire goals development system is based on people's personal goals for income, and if you do that first, you can succeed as a performance-driven sales manager.

The reason so many people don't believe in setting goals for themselves is that they have no coach, no personal mentor to help them set them and achieve them. They're in it by themselves and become victim to outside influences who share their point of view. Too many people work from a mental position of lack, of not having enough. That's the background music of their lives, and, predictably, lack follows them through life. When you find these people on your sales staff, it is up to you to help them arrive at a point of epiphany where their personal paradigm changes from one of lack to one of abundance.

## Make a Coaching Agreement with Your Salespeople

Thanks to what you now know about how to use sales metrics, you are in a unique position to lead each person on your staff to their personal goal. However, to be successful in this endeavor, you have to establish and maintain a coaching relationship with each person. These partnerships for performance form the crux of sales management in businesses where individual sales performance dictates the company's results.

Remember, *all* sales revenue moves through your salespeople, and nothing else you do as a manager is as important as getting maximum sales revenue from every customer opportunity.

Your salespeople have to believe you know what you're talking about and what you're doing. If you do not provide a clearly defined company selling strategy that is based on solid consumer research, actual performance metrics, and common sense, your efforts to get people to work in certain ways will be viewed by salespeople as being just your opinion about how they should work. They'll see your efforts to change how they work as mere suggestions, or interference, instead of direction. They will tell you this outright when challenged, insisting, "That won't work for me" or "That doesn't sound like me"; when you're teaching them to use scripted dialogs, they'll say, "We'll all sound the same."

I've laid out earlier in this book this "nothing fails like success" syndrome; because they have successfully closed a lot of sales using different methods and techniques from those you're asking them to apply, they want to keep doing it their way. Their old selling skills have worked just enough times for them to keep using them, and the result is they miss all of the potential buyers who need a little more help, or a lot more help, and they therefore place a limit on their earnings. You have to help them change their thinking.

### The Process

Give your staff a report on all of the information and the strategic development process. Do it as a special staff meeting off site and off hours, if possible. Make it a special occasion and require attendance. Let those salespeople who were part of the development process make presentations, so everyone knows salespeople were represented and involved in the process. Open the floor to questions, and resolve every one of them. If you can't resolve an issue or answer a question, place it in a "parking lot" until you achieve resolutions, then communicate the resolutions to everyone.

Next, meet with each person independently and agree on all the things you and they will do in this partnership to achieve their goals. Sales managers serve two masters: the company and the salespeople. You cannot achieve your company's goals unless your salespeople achieve their personal goals, so your concentration has to be on the salespeople. Document the agreement in writing so there is no question about your commitment or theirs.

Salespeople will:

&raquo; Take full accountability for each customer opportunity

» Document each opportunity using your Room Design Profile

» Enter each opportunity into your sales management or Customer Relationship Management system, such as Trax®.

» Greet and serve according to your company selling system

» Sketch every room

» Offer more help through room-planning services to encourage Be-Backs and improve close ratio and average sale

» Maintain daily action (to-do) lists and report to you on completion

» Complete all customer project work on schedule

» Follow up with non-buyers to encourage Be-Backs

» Achieve close ratio of 30 percent of total opportunities

» Achieve average sale of $1,786

» Achieve a minimum 15 percent ratio of Be-Backs to total opportunities each month

» Maintain long-term contact using e-mail, regular mail, and other follow up methods that your customer has agreed to.

» Meet weekly with you to review progress toward their monthly and annual goals

You will:

» Monitor all sales activity throughout each day

» Maintain daily month-to-date (MTD) reports on sales performance for each individual and for the team

» Provide daily feedback to each person on their MTD performance

» Provide daily total store MTD performance feedback to the team

» Identify performance weaknesses and provide immediate one-to-one or group training as required

» Coach each person to ensure that all work activity is directed toward achieving their personal goals

» Monitor all action lists on a daily basis to ensure the highest level of Be-Back customers

» Monitor all design project work and keep them on track

## Aligning Company Financial Goals with Salespeople's Personal Goals

The company will have developed goals from a budgetary standpoint, and in our continuing example, we're targeting $5,940,000, an increase of $1,140,000 over last year's revenue. This is not a "blue-sky" goal that management made up out of the air, but an amount based on improving the performance of those people who are below the store average in close ratio and average sale. That requires no additional advertising expenditures and no higher level of customer traffic than the previous year or goal period.

As described above, if each person on your staff is willing to commit to generating $833,300 in net sales, and to follow your prescribed formula for opportunities (1,560), close ratio (30 percent), and average sale ($1,780), you need only seven salespeople on your staff to get you there. However, if your traffic tracking system has shown 20,000 shoppers came through your doors last year, and you're projecting, a 20 percent decline to 16,000 due to economic conditions, you have to account for coverage to serve every one of those shoppers. 16,000 divided by 1,560 = 10.3 salespeople, so you'll have 10 full-time salespeople on your staff. This way, you've staffed for maximum customer coverage on weekends and now, if everyone were to achieve their $50,000 goal from 1,560 opportunities, you store sales will be $8,333,000! A typically understaffed store that does not count actual consumer traffic in total or by salesperson, would completely miss this $2,393,000 opportunity by remaining grossly understaffed.

A typical scenario when the total sales/income goals of your staff amount to less than your store goals is no to change anyone's goals; their goals are what they're willing to commit to, not the company's goals. Instead, companies add more salespeople. Of course, this depends on each person's stated income goal being acceptable based on them achieving the expected revenue per opportunity at the expected performance levels for opportunities, close ratio, average sale, Be-Backs, and room-planning projects.

Whatever income people want for themselves has to be derived, in our example, from 1,560 customer opportunities per year, or 130 per month on average. Your number of opportunities per salesperson may be different from this model depending on how you structure your selling strategy. In our case, you've elected to use a very high service strategy, and therefore have aligned everything to that strategy. You may choose to follow a different model from what I've set out here, but the point is that you've based it all on data, not on guessing about what's happening in your store.

## The Goal Development Meeting

When you meet with your salesperson, be fully prepared to set realistic goals. Have a record of this person's earnings for the last few years, which you get from your company's payroll records or from asking them about earnings from previous jobs. Have their actual performance records showing results over 90 days or longer; this provides their actual sales success equation for the time they've been working with you. Don't hold these meetings until you are fully prepared with all necessary information.

You want to know two things from this meeting: First, what is the weekly, monthly, or annual earnings amount that will make an immediate improvement in this person's quality of life; and, second, how committed are they to achieving it?

You want to be sure that the goal is achievable if the person does all the things required to make it happen. You need early successes to keep the process alive. There will be a simple back-and-forth around all the data you have, all the behaviors you've witnessed, their feelings and motivations, and the new initiatives you've developed to help your salespeople perform better for themselves, your company, and your customers.

## Summary

This discussion of goals really boils down to the fact that you, your company, and your salespeople can all achieve your goals if you help more customers achieve their goals. Goals are achieved — or not — based on how your salespeople interact with your customers and your selling strategy. All of the tactical initiatives you've developed are aimed at enhancing the quality of that relationship, and income/sales goals are the manifestation of the salesperson's stake in your strategic sales plan.

Goals management means that you, the leader on the floor, take accountability for developing individual road maps to your salespeople's goals. The next thing you will do is to monitor their performance — their progress along the mapped-out route — and keep them on the right course.

# Chapter 13

## Leadership and Coaching on the Selling Floor: A Guide for Sales Managers

## Introduction

Think about a professional sports team and its management structure. Head coaches or field managers are at every game, on the sidelines, observing performance. There are veritable teams of other coaches and observers watching the game being played, reporting play-by-play details of performance. The team of subordinate coaches suggests adjustments to how the game is being played at the moment, as compared to the game plan or overall strategy that the team employs. In football, where all individual assignments are spelled out in detail and the observers report to the "team" of the head coach, the defensive coordinator, and offensive coordinator on how well the game plan is going, adjustments are made immediately.

The head coach isn't back in his office working on the travel plans for next week's game or looking at video of past games. He's not working on ensuring that there are enough hot dogs at the concession stands or selling team hats in the stadium shops. He's not working on recruiting the next phenomenal player. He's right there, on the field managing the game.

You selling strategy is your playbook. The dialogs, sketches, room plans, and other engagement tools are like individual plays you run to make a sale. You have a strategy; you have well-trained salespeople and great tools to support them, and you have customers out there. The question is, where's the coach?

You need to be on the field of play every day, all day. This is your primary job, to manage the game as it's played and to do the one thing none of the sports coaches can do – actually play. You can actually participate in the playing of the game. You can get right in there with customers and salespeople and demonstrate how to "play" — that is, prompt behaviors, like sketching and room planning, for your salespeople. You can show customers that in your store, management cares about them and about the salespeople. You can demonstrate teamwork, a commitment to high levels of service, and a customer-centered engagement strategy, but the trick is to do it without looking like you're undermining the salesperson.

Not having full-time management presence on the floor is one of the deadliest mistakes most retailers make. Your game is a complicated one: You have a complex, skill-centered selling strategy that requires constant coaching to ensure compliance, yet few stores insist that managers get involved in the game. In fact, most stores require so much back-end support and sales order management from their sales managers that it's impossible for them to coach on the floor. In a strategic selling system, it is absolutely essential that sales managers work on the selling floor. This is particularly important on weekends, when more than half of each week's shoppers are in your store. I call Saturday and Sunday Game Days. This is when you must be out there with your team executing your selling strategy and locking customers into your products and services.

There are two kinds of coaching required of sales manager in retail stores where one-to-one, customer-to-salesperson relationships are the selling format: Situational coaching on the selling floor, and strategic coaching in a one-to-one environment.

## Setting the Stage

Begin each day with a morning huddle. Set the stage by planning how you will together handle the day's traffic. Remind your team of the main goals for the day, and how you will work with them to achieve everyone's goals for the day. Here's one suggestion for planning a weekend day:

> *"I'll be on the floor with you all day today. I'll be approaching you as you engage customers and I'll be looking for two things: Customer names and room sketches. When I approach you, please pause, and introduce me by name to your customers and tell me their names. You should have all this on your Room Design Profile. Tell me what room they're working on and where you are in the process of understanding their needs.*

> *"If you don't have a sketch, I'm going to ask your customer to tell me about their room, and if the situation is right, I'll do a sketch with them. You stay right there and be prepared to take over when I'm done.*

> *"I'll try not to get too involved or appear to have more knowledge than you so I don't destroy your credibility. Besides, you're more knowledgeable about all this than I am anyway. I'm just trying to guide you into our selling process.*

> *"When I leave you and your customers, I'll say something nice about you and your ability to*

*solve their problem. Please live up to the promise I make for you.*

*"After your customer leaves, if they don't purchase today, I'll be looking for your Be-Back appointment or follow-up plan and contact information on the Room Design Profile."*

## Handling Heavy Traffic Periods

On special sale days or holidays, you can easily be overwhelmed with traffic, even when you are staffed correctly. When this happens, position yourself at the front door as the greeter for all shoppers and be the "traffic cop" for your salespeople. This is the best place for you to be in times of overflow so you get to deal with all those un-served customers.

Greet everyone. Unattended customers are not good for your business, so apologize for not having anyone available to them and ensure them you'll get them attention as soon as possible. Introduce yourself and ask for their names and make a note of them right then and there. Let them see you do it. If you have a few minutes to ask and answer some simple questions, make notes of what you discussed. Do not get involved in serving them as their salesperson, because as soon as you do you're lost to the rest of those overflow customers who come in afterwards. Ask an open question like, "What room are you working on?" or "What brings you in today?" so you can know who needs help first. Consider this triage for sales. You'll learn who the "hot" customers are and be able to direct your salespeople to those who are most likely to buy or to seek connection. If you find yourself in this position often, think about adding salespeople.

Have your salespeople come to you for direction to their next opportunity. Try to not just point your salesperson in the direction of the customer, but actually take him there and make an introduction. This keeps you in control of the floor and keeps your salespeople targeted on the most viable customers. In addition, they always know where you are in times of overflow. Managers I've worked who have trouble doing this are usually tied up behind the front desk dealing with the minutia of sales order entry, financing, inventory issues, and other non-sales producing activities. Sales order administration is the job of administrators. If you have an assistant sales manager, office manager, or other such support help, assign them to the front desk where they can best apply their administrative skills in support of salespeople.

Never forget that the first mission of retail salespeople and sales managers is to close sales. Don't let anything get in the way of closing sales. Writing sales is secondary to closing them, and while there are many reasons why salespeople have to be involved in the process, there are ways to make it easier for them and for your customers. By making the actual writing of the sales an administrative function placed in the hands of experts whose only task is to complete the sales transaction, you will greatly reduce the number of errors and enhance overall customer satisfaction. The overhead costs of a few sales order entry clericals is the limiting factor, but I believe this can be offset by the benefits to customer service and accuracy, and increase the productive use of salesperson's time.

## Observation and Intervention

As you tour your selling floor and observe your salespeople and their customers, you should be aware of the overall feeling of the floor, its general demeanor and atmosphere. Hopefully, the floor is alive with people, all of whom are involved in the complex web of communications and ideas. Customers have pictures in their heads of their home and the room their working on today. Salespeople are trying to understand that picture and somehow qualify and quantify the customer's needs. You need to be aware of this web of communication and be able to evaluate its quality and nature, because they way you feel about it is the way your customers are feeling about it. So as you tour around you store on a busy afternoon, ask yourself frequently, "How does this feel?"

When you join a salesperson/customer engagement, always smile and wait for the salesperson to introduce you. It should be as natural, welcoming, and friendly as if their best friend just stopped by. He should introduce you by name. If he doesn't, simply smile happily and say to the customer, "I'm Joe Capillo, I'm the sales manager. You are...?" When the customer responds, you've performed a wonderful coaching lesson live, on the floor.

If he can tell you what room or project his customer is working on, and what he's learned about what they're shopping for, just say something nice like, "That's great, we have over 100 sofas to choose from, and I know Charles will help you find just the right one for your room. You're in good hands."

If Charles can't tell you anything about his customer's room or needs, you need to go to work. This demonstration of your selling system is critically important to Charles and all his associates on the floor. Ask for his Room Design Profile and say to the customer:

> *"Well, you're in the right place for sofas; we have over 100 different looks on display. I'm sure we can help you make a great selection, but we really need to know more about your issues, so please tell us about your room and what you're trying to accomplish today."*

When you sketch the room, you'll have to stay connected a little longer — it doesn't come across well if you just sketch and walk away — so make a few suggestions and get out of the engagement as soon as you can. You do not want the customers to see you as capable and Charles as unknowledgeable. If this does happen, a valuable lesson is available for Charles to learn, and you should deal with it another time in an off-the-floor coaching session.

This is called modeling performance. Showing your salespeople how to apply the various aspects of your selling system.

## Situational Coaching

When you go onto the floor to observe and intervene in this manner be sure you know your dialogs and don't vary from them. If you do, you destroy all of your strategic planning, and the standard of performance will become vague and open to interpretation — the last thing you want to happen.

You strategic selling plan spells out the standard of performance from greeting to closing, and on to follow-up communications to maintain customer relationships. Make sure you know it and perform to that standard when you're modeling performance on the floor.

Managers who work this way on the floor shorten the learning curve for salespeople by doing what they do, dealing with their issues, and handling the same customers they handle. This is the most powerful teaching tool you have and you should make sure you get involved this way with every salesperson on your staff.

## Effective Feedback for Change

When you are engaged on the floor with salespeople and customers, hold all your feedback and input regarding the salesperson's performance until after the customer has left the store. It is, however, important to react immediately to things you see and hear that are off track with your selling strategy — or that are blatantly wrong. This is the hardest thing to do, believe me. I've had to do it and hold my temper in check countless times, but don't correct or embarrass your salesperson in the presence of a customer.

Even when you're there observing and listening, remain silent until you can take the salesperson aside after the customer has left your store. I always ask the salesperson one question, "How could that engagement have been better?" More often than not, they know the answer, but when they don't you have a great opportunity to teach against the backdrop of a real situation that you witnessed. I never tell a person what she did wrong, but I recreate the situation, let's say a customer asked a question about a product or service and the salesperson answered incorrectly or incompletely. In this case, too, you have an opportunity to teach by simply asking her to look at her training material and tell you what should, or could, have happened.

When you witness a lack of product knowledge, you can help your salesperson do some targeted learning on a product category or vendor. When you see and hear a poorly executed dialog, you know you have to provide more practice training. This will occur mostly around the dialogs for selling room planning, house calls, and warranties that you develop in your selling strategy meetings.

Coaching, modeling, and directing on the floor is a critical sales manager function in any selling system where salespeople deal directly with one customer at a time and all sales must go through a salesperson. You have to show and not just tell. Remember, words do not teach; actions teach. Being involved on the selling floor and modeling desired behaviors teaches your salespeople how to successfully apply the things they've been taught. Your goal is simply to show how to connect to those relational customers and make sure those transactional customers come back again.

# CHAPTER 14

# THE ART OF COACHING FOR ACHIEVING GOALS

## Introduction

I'll repeat something important here: you don't manage groups, teams, or forces. You coach individuals. It is not necessary to manage people; they need to manage themselves. People need leadership and coaching to achieve their personal goals. I see this as the core of every sales manager's role, because without each person performing at a high level, you cannot consistently achieve your store's goals. When you look at the range of performance of any sales staff in overall sales and in the three critical factors, you'll typically find that the top person performs as much as 67 percent better than the lowest-performing person. This is where your potential sales growth lies, not in bringing new shoppers through the door.

Have a weekly, fifteen-minute, one-to-one meeting with each salesperson to review the past week's results and where they are now relative to their monthly and annual goals. You have a variety of tools at your disposal to understand what happened last week and set plans for next week.

» Your goal development plan, which shows where each person should be in number of opportunities, close ratio, and average sale.

» By using electronic up-boards like Trax®, you have a detailed record of every opportunity logged by the salesperson.

» You have category sales reports from your operating system by salesperson, and with an electronic up-board you have a record of the number of customer opportunities each salesperson had for each category you've defined.

» You have a Room Design Profile form for every opportunity so that you can see customer contact information, room sketches, merchandise needs, follow-up plans, and Be-Back appointments (if any).

» You have notes from your observation on the floor.

» You have category sales results from your operating system.

» With most electronic up-boards, each person receives a daily feedback report on where they stand for the month-to-date versus their sales goals, so there should not be any surprises for them at any weekly meeting.

» You have payroll information to track their year-to-date earnings, which are the crux of this whole strategy — help them earn what they want to earn.

You have more detailed information about individual performance than any sales manager in history. You can see patterns and trends using salespeople's written records in the Room Design Profile, the most direct documentation for every customer engagement. These are reviewed by you each day for all customer engagements. In Trax®, you also review each day's customer transaction records as your salespeople enter them. Throughout each day, you can look at all transactions entered so far at any time. This is not micromanaging; it's micromonitoring, and I believe that it is a necessary daily function for sales managers.

## Merchandise Category Sales Tracking – Beware Percentages

The first place I look when a salesperson has a performance problem and is not achieving goals is the category sales record. Virtually all operating systems provide this data on demand. You know the overall category sales breakdown for the retail furniture industry from NHFA operating reports. You know your store's sales history by category. Using your sales management software, Trax or others, you now also know the breakdown of your store's shoppers by category because your salespeople report this data for each opportunity.

Let's say your store's breakdown of sales by category looks like this:

| | |
|---|---|
| All upholstery types | 40 percent |
| Bedroom | 20 percent |
| Dining (all) | 10 percent |
| Bedding | 10 percent |
| Occasional | 5 percent |
| Home Office | 5 percent |
| Accessories + | 7 percent |
| Non-furniture | 3 percent |
| Total | 100 percent |

There is only 100 percent to work with. You cannot have sales of more or less than 100 percent; it's the absolute limit. Your dollar sales could double and your percentage breakdown could still look exactly like this. Using percentages of total sales to determine a salesperson's effectiveness is wrong. If a person is low in one category, simple math shows they must be high in at least one other category. The only way to legitimately compare effectiveness in category performance is by sales dollars.

I am always amused by reports that use percentage of sales as a comparison for category performance of stores.

The thinking, or I should say non-thinking, seems to be that if one store is performing at 15 percent of total sales in bedding and another is at 10 percent, the former is performing better than the latter. This is mathematical nonsense.

With the technology you have available to track all opportunities, you now have a record of the actual number of sales opportunities each salesperson gets for each category. Because it is mathematically likely that your store's shopping traffic breakdown by category looks much like your category sales breakdown, and because you provide equal opportunities for all salespeople, it's also mathematically likely that everyone gets the same percentage, and number, of customers for each category, over time.

This logically leads to the conclusion that if the store achieves 15 percent of sales in the bedroom category but one salesperson is performing at, say, 10 percent of sales in this category, then your store and this salesperson are losing sales. The good news is that with your sales activity tracked electronically, as with Trax®, you can see the number of bedroom opportunities logged by the salesperson over your review period — let's say, one quarter — and extract category dollar sales for the same period from your operating system. If the opportunities are relatively equal to all other salespeople, and the dollars sold are much lower, you have a problem you can address and solve.

The reason you look first at category performance is because you can solve these problems easily since they generally revolve around merchandise knowledge and product presentation issues. Before you try to fix a sales process problem, you have to fix the knowledge and presentation problems.

## Coach to the Standard of Performance

The beauty of having a documented selling system based on strategic research and your company's specific market is that you have a standard for how salespeople should work with customers that everyone knows and understands. There is no "opinion" about how salespeople should work, and you don't have to deal with a number of different beliefs or individual paradigms around how salespeople think they should engage customers.

Your observations, measurements, and inspection of daily work will show you where each individual is off track.

> If you review ten Room Design Profiles and find no room sketches, the person isn't doing his job as called for in your selling strategy — and you have the solution.

> If you check the electronic activity calendar and find no follow-up contacts scheduled, the salesperson is off-strategy — and you have the solution.

> If your computer performance reports show a low number and percentage of Be-Back opportunities, the person is off-track — and you have the solution.

> If a salesperson has no Room Planning projects underway, she's off-track — and you have the solution.

> If the salesperson is not achieving their goals for income and sales, they know they're off-track — and you and they have the solution.

You have everything you need to help you help each salesperson perform better, sell more, and earn more. With all this information and your written selling plan, all you have to do is demonstrate where an individual's performance varies from the standard, obtain their agreement, reflect upon your goal achievement agreement, and offer suggestions for improvement.

## Coach to the Metrics

Each person has a personal sales success equation based on receiving 130 customer opportunities per month. (Your standard may be higher or lower than this, but nothing changes in how you deal with the numbers.) Your first place to look in coaching for improved performance has to be at the number of opportunities a person has had so far in the month.

If they're tracking at the rate of 130 per month (total number received ÷ number of days worked x number of workdays remaining), you next want to look at the number and percentage of Be-Back customers they've had so far. If the monthly opportunities are tracking over 130, don't do anything. If they're tracking behind the 130 level, look at everyone else's numbers and overall traffic. This is putting first things first and taking accountability for the one factor in the sales success equation that is company based. But remember: There's a fundamental rule in this method of management: When traffic drops, close ratio and average sale have to go up — or else everyone loses ground.

Review the range of performance to determine if your top performers are still on top. Look at the Revenue per Opportunity for your most effective and least effective performers. Compare this number to your 90-day running average.

Next look at the person's current month close ratio compared to their 90-day running close ratio. If the number is comparatively low, then Be-Backs may be the problem. If it's higher, move on to average sale.

Average sale is a "spiking" metric; it can move up and down dramatically from month-to-month depending on things like promotions, holidays, season, and economic influences. This is why it's so important to maintain a running 90-day average for your overall metrics and individual performances. Compare this person's number to that of your best performers for this month and to your store average over the same period.

Determine your approach prior to meeting with each salesperson. They are either on target according to their sales success equation, or they're not, and the reasons are now obvious and quantifiable.

## Provide Uplifting, Relevant, and Timely Feedback

Coaching is an uplifting discipline, not a critical one. Consider these two approaches to the same performance problem:

*1.*
*"John, your performance is not up to standard. You're way behind for the month, and we have to fix this fast because you're costing us business. I don't see nearly enough room sketches for the number of opportunities you've had, and you have no room-planning projects in process. Your number of Be-Backs is dismal, to say the least. I'm really disappointed in you, so here's what I want you to do..."*

*2.*
*"John, give me your take on the month so far."*
*Then listen.*

*"OK, I agree it's been a difficult month so far for you. What's your solution?"*

*"I understand all you want to do, but let's make this simple and do one thing at a time. Let's take the simplest path to help you get back on track. I think you're trying too hard to close sales and aren't spending enough time listening to you customers — I've seen this happen when I was out on the floor with you yesterday. Let's look at a couple of your Room Design Profiles for*

*this week and discuss how things might have gone better. Then we can decide how to proceed, OK?"*

*"OK, you obviously understand the selling system, so let's do this: Go out there and get one sketch today, just one. All you have to do is say 'Tell me about your room' — it's that simple. Do all the things we've talked about and let's see what happens. Come back and see me when you get that sketch."*

The last example is a partnership approach. The coach didn't rage at the person, but took a softer approach and took the path of reviewing actual situations instead of simply repeating strategic dogma. She referenced "yesterday" as a current observation and offered just one, simple suggestion for a short time period. Something the salesperson can accomplish without too much stress. When the salesperson does this, it will be a small victory in coaching, regardless of what the outcome is with the customer.

## Develop Performance Improvement Plans

Performance improvement plans should not be for longer than one week. It's important to work with a time frame short enough so that all customer engagements are current. There's no sense trying to discuss something that happened more than a few days ago. Don't make performance improvement plans that you don't follow up. Fill your calendar with scheduled meetings with salespeople. In fact, post this calendar in the sales office for all to see, and never, ever miss a meeting.

Performance Improvement Plans have to actually mean something to everyone involved. Remember, I warned that at the beginning of your goals management process, you'll be more interested in your people's goals than they are, because people without leaders drift.

Make sure you celebrate every victory, small or large. Celebrate each successful application of your strategy. Keep criticism private. Keep your people informed of how the store is doing overall, no matter how bad things are. There is no requirement that you as a sales manager have to motivate anyone. Motivation is an internal emotion, just as attitude is a choice.

## Summary

Take the high road in coaching at all times. Never forget that you are in the salesperson business, not in the customer business. That's the salesperson's job. Your role relative to customers is to develop, train, and oversee the delivery of services that help them achieve their goals for beautiful homes and an enhanced quality of life.

Your salespeople will achieve their goals to the extent they help customers achieve *their* goals. You will achieve your store goals to the extent salespeople achieve their personal sales goals. Your sales and sales management strategies are in complete alignment to achieve everyone's goals.

# MAINTAINING STRATEGIC ALIGNMENT FOR PERFORMANCE IMPROVEMENT

## Introduction

For business owners and managers, keeping your organization aligned toward achieving top-line sales goals is too often overlooked as a management imperative, but it's the most prevalent point of failure in most companies. It requires a full-time commitment by the leaders in every company discipline in order for it to happen. John Kotter, of Harvard Business School, writes in his book *Leading Change*[7], that the number two reason for failure of change initiatives in companies is the lack of a supportive, committed coalition at the top. The number one reason is because management allows too much complacency by top-echelon officers, department heads, and front-line employees. I read this book in 1996 and have never read any other business book with more relevant advice regarding why initiatives fail — and how to do it right.

Among Kotter's other top reasons for the failure of strategic initiatives are:

» Failure to communicate the new *vision* to all members of the company every day in every way

- ❧ Underestimating the length of time such changes take to become part of the company's culture — declaring victory too soon
- ❧ Failure to create short-term wins and leveraging them for more wins
- ❧ Allowing obstacles to block the new vision
- ❧ Not anchoring the new vision solidly in the corporate culture

No matter how small or large your company is, I know you have seen this kind of cultural inertia in your organizations. The strategic vision of this book is that you can help your stores, and our industry, change the way you interact with consumers, providing a new level of service that addresses real problems people have solving home design problems.

To successfully transform your company, you need a coalition of leaders who are fully committed to improving sales and profits on a full-time basis. In small organizations, it's expected that these people work in the business on their respective "firing lines," but you also have to make time for them to work on the business at the strategic level as I've shown. When there is no one working on the business, you are sure to stagnate and not be responsive to today's lightning-fast market changes. In other words, this is not your father or grandfather's business.

## Define Your Vision

Write down you vision of what your company will be like, look like, and feel like, after your new selling strategy (or any strategic initiative) is part of your everyday lives. How do you see your company enhanced by this initiative? How will it be a better place to shop, to work, to manage and to own? This is an extension of your mission (see Chapter 3), and it answers all these questions. Get help with this from all your executives and those people who participate in the strategic development process.

Your vision is not limited to improving sales revenue, which is the core issue addressed by this book, but also includes all areas of revenue and expense including finance, administration, systems, operations, merchandising and purchasing, advertising and promotion, and facilities management.

The financial condition of your company is reported on your balance sheet, and that is where the owners and financial officers need to live. The other department heads live in areas whose results feed the balance sheet. An example is the direct relationship between inventory and cash. Your merchandise manager and buyers need to understand the affect of GMROI on cash, meaning they have to balance the need for customer satisfaction with inventory turns and gross margin. They have to make inventory available when customers need it, but they should not store inventory for long periods, tying up cash and limiting the company's ability to react to market changes and opportunities.

Advertising and promotion have to balance their goal of maintaining customer traffic at required levels, while being sensitive to the need to maintain gross margin and to stay within the budgetary limitations for production and media expense. They also have to communicate the sales service strategy to potential customers, drawing in both relational and transactional customers, who may respond to different messages.

In small companies, most top-level managers may have two or three jobs, all of which are interdependent in optimizing all financial results. This points to the need for a robust, fully integrated operating system with powerful reporting functionality, and to the importance of using your system's total functionality.

## Communicate Your Vision Repeatedly

This is the talk-the-talk and walk-the-walk part of making your new strategic selling plan work and of achieving those big sales gains we calculated in Chapter 2. This is where the work of day-to-day management and on-the-floor leadership pays off. This is where you see and feel your vision brought to life and your mission accomplished.

## The Power of Goals

In sales, implementing all of the aspects of whichever sales management system you use is critical in getting everyone to pay attention every day. This is why regular feedback on performance versus goals is extremely important. Celebrating each small or large victory in the new selling system is paramount to leveraging exciting outcomes into more strategic compliance with your new selling system.

## Accountability for Performance at the Top

You can use the same process laid out in Chapter 3 to document your strategic plan and to drive continued strategic and tactical changes on the selling floor. Your management team is your leadership team, and they all need to be fully involved throughout your implementation of new strategies, no matter which organizational aspect is the subject. This is the way you implement and secure changes in each and every aspect of your business. It's simple to do and to understand.

To keep a new strategic initiative alive after you've invested time and intellectual effort to create it, make sure every department has something to do in the initial stages. For example:

> ❧ The sales department obviously has the mission of implementing the new sales strategy. Their

department goal is to improve overall revenue per shopper by increasing your close ratio and average sale. They will do this by performing room-planning project work with customers, so their individual goal is to develop qualified projects with an additional two percent of your total customer opportunities, and to increase the percentage of Be-Back shoppers to a minimum of 15 percent of the total number of opportunities.

» Merchandising and purchasing might have similar responsibilities to reduce excess inventory, improve GMROI, and re-display the selling floor to show more complete room settings in support of a room-based selling strategy.

» Advertising has the mission of developing ad campaigns that both support the new strategy and attract both transactional and relational shoppers.

» The delivery department has the mission of creating training for delivery crews and customer service people to reflect them being them being the people who deliver not just the furniture but also the promise.

As you define each strategic project, you will develop short-term, or milestone, goals that, when achieved, move the project forward. There might be dozens of such milestones that are dependency goals, meaning that the next step can't be achieved until the milestones are achieved. An example is that you will not succeed in developing room-planning projects until sketching rooms becomes an institutional part of the selling process. Therefore, the number of sketched rooms by salespeople could be a milestone goal. Likewise, you can't improve your close ratio dramatically unless you improve the number of Be-Back shoppers to at least 15 percent of total shoppers, so you might have a milestone goal of improving the percentage of Be-Back shoppers from your baseline of, say, five percent to 10 percent in one month (it can happen that fast).

Document each department's first milestone and time goals on sticky notes as discussed in Chapter 3. I like to move these sticky notes to a flip chart page for each department and attach them to the meeting room wall so they remain in plain sight and are there for the next meeting. In the early stages of a project, I suggest keeping the time periods for early goals short and attainable; start off slowly to ensure some early success that can be leveraged forward.

When you look at the work of your people in this way, you see the alignment of all work initiatives into a single strategic approach to your business. Your leadership initiative is to keep some part of your department managers' work directed at implementing new initiatives while also maintaining current operations under those "old" ways that work and support the new ways.

Transition periods are difficult, and you have to introduce new methods with caution and not declare success too soon. Finally, you have to ensure that the new strategies, methods, systems, and procedures become "the way we do things" instead of the "new idea" de jour. If you allow complacency to take over — if your people only congratulate themselves on the great plans but fail to implement them — you will fail in your efforts to change your company's direction.

## Holding Effective Project Status Meetings

These are my suggestions for holding short, effective strategy team meetings to keep everyone involved and informed about the status of the strategic initiative.

❧ Keep your meetings short and focused only on department reports of progress in the execution of new initiatives.

» Work from a pre-distributed written agenda. Allow time for managers to suggest agenda changes prior to the meeting.

» Set your first few meetings weekly; you can change this later.

» Assign a facilitator to keep the meeting on focus and on time. This can be anyone involved on the strategic development team and can rotate from meeting to meeting. However, in small family businesses, I like to have the principal operating owner as the overall project leader.

» They either achieved them or not.

» When goals are achieved, be congratulatory and supportive.

» When goals are not achieved, simply deal with the reasons, review the viability of the goal, change it if necessary, and set a new time goal.

» Use sticky notes to document all new goals, action items, initiatives, and adjourn.

With your changes documented and next-step milestones in place, make sure your departmental goals for the next meeting are clear and agreeable to everyone. If there need to be specific actions performed, write them down, distribute them, and post them. Write the action items down for each project team leader, and ensure that everyone on the team remains informed as to how they can assist each other to achieve their goals. There are always interdependencies among departments in projects like these.

Keep your action items live by using a tool such as Outlook to retain task lists, milestone dates, and to schedule all future meetings, conference calls, etc. If all participants are in one work location, you can have them update their project sheets as they complete action items. There are several Project Management software programs that can electronically document these processes, but the learning curve is long and I find their use like using an atom bomb to kill a fly. Keep things simple.

## Management Team Meetings for Performance Accountability

Your new strategic selling system is now part of your company's culture. You're making some progress toward your goals for improving average sale, close ratio and revenue per opportunity, and you're ready to declare your implementation project successful. Don't do it. Anyone who remembers Murphy's Law will recall the second corollary: Everything takes longer than you think it will. The law itself states, "Anything that can go wrong, will, and at the most inopportune time with the maximum negative affect."

Weekly management team meetings are vital in a retail setting where the game is on all day, every day your stores are open. When you meet weekly and review month-to-date performance, you have three chances to make necessary changes. If you meet only monthly, you have no chance to agree on strategic or operational adjustments to your game plan for the current month. Weekly management team meetings also help you maintain a high level of urgency, which is necessary in a fast-moving retail environment.

Your sales managers' report for your weekly meeting might cover the following things:

- ❧ A review of individual and group performance to date; sales management systems such as Trax® provide a variety of reports to use
- ❧ Traffic reviews for this period versus last year, last month, expectations
- ❧ Staffing updates
- ❧ Number of room-planning projects in process by type (in-store or house call) and by salesperson
- ❧ New room-planning projects by salesperson and as

a percentage of total opportunities
- » Review of how each salesperson is doing relative to their income goals
- » Category sales reports (shared with merchandising department head)
  - » Number of customer opportunities by category
  - » Percentage of category shoppers to total opportunities

At least one weekly meeting each month should be devoted to reviewing the previous month's income statement for monthly and year-to-date results compared to goals and budgets. Profitability is a 12-step program and, because there is nothing more important to the company than being financially healthy, this means monthly monitoring by the executive or management team.

I find this to be one of the weaknesses among small businesses in our industry, because while all of the widely used operating systems provide monthly financial reports, many businesses don't take advantage of this opportunity to stay on track. You can't make fast enough adjustments to expenses when you see your financial statements months down the road. This high level of monitoring also keeps your management team focused on the strategic plan and on their respective departmental goals in the framework of the actual effect on the financial health of your company, an important link in your overall success.

# CONCLUSION

I've witnessed a lot of successful companies in the home furnishings industry as well as a lot of failures. Some of the biggest companies in home furnishings retailing have failed within the past decade. Levitz and Homelife (formerly Sears Furniture Division) failed for many reasons, but key among them is that they maintained outdated strategies far too long in a changing marketplace.

As the manufacturing and distribution of home furnishings has expanded into a global enterprise, moving away from its initial localized nature, all of us have had to adapt, and this is the failing point for many small, independent companies. Our industry has not been very sophisticated in its application of consumer research to our daily operations. That's partly because no small business can afford the cost of such research. There are now many sources available, however, in our information-based universes, and I urge you to take advantage of them in your decision-making.

Throughout this book, we have followed a strategic line of thinking and action to develop more customer-centered systems. I believe that every retail home furnishings company could benefit from the application of a room-based selling system, whether it becomes the core system, or as added services, but you have to do more than just offer free design services. You have to see the added sales potential and customer retention possibilities of this kind of high-service orientation, and you can only do that by knowing all of the key sales metrics of your company.

Execution is always the point of failure for strategic plans, and I've offered ways for you to overcome the usual blockades to implementation by maintaining high-level management accountability for performance. There's an old saying that if you want to make God laugh, tell Him your plans. Nonetheless, without growth, you will surely fail, and in a fast-changing world, growth won't always come through an ever-expanding market.

The methods I've provided are effective for small businesses and don't require very expensive technology to employ. Listen to your customers and serve their underlying needs if you want to achieve customer loyalty. Earn the right to be fully connected and engaged in the needs your customers have for beautiful, comfortable, well-designed rooms and homes, and maintain a strategic view of your relationship with them.

# APPENDICES

## Appendix A
### A Sample 15-Day New Hire Training Plan

## Appendix B
### Room Design Profile Form

## Appendix C
### Floor Product Audit Process & Form

## Appendix D
### Room Design Information Workbook

**Visit our website at
www.JoeCapillo.com/SolutionStore
to download these forms in PDF format.**

## Appendix A
## A Sample 15-Day New Hire Training Plan

### DAY ONE

**MORNING**     Sales manager/HR manager

❧ HR orientation, necessary employment forms, benefits review

❧ Company organization chart, chain of communications, policies, rules & regulations

❧ Person-to-person introductions if possible. List of all key executives, managers, workflow for order processing and delivery system.

**AFTERNOON**

❧ Introduce your sales mission — this is important to all that follows

❧ Customer engagement strategy introduction and overview — fundamental concepts

❧ Assign reading of selling system textbook
   » Give them reading time in the store

❧ Set review schedule to handle questions, get feedback, and connect training to you sales mission

### DAY TWO

**MORNING**     Sales Manager

❧ Review one or two chapters from reading materials on customer engagement strategy

❧ Ask new hires to tell you what they understand to be the message of the customer engagement program

**AFTERNOON** Sales manager, assistant sales manager

❧ Introduction to your computer operating system

❧ Introduction to other key systems such as Icovia® or Trax®

### DAY THREE

**MORNING**     Sales manager

» Vendor overview — top 10 vendor list
» Speak to who provides which products, price ranges — good, better, best layout
» Tour floor briefly
» Set product category overview
» Describe self-learning floor audit process

**AFTERNOON** Sales manager, or assistant sales manager, or office manager

» Computer training

## DAY FOUR

**MORNING** Self-learning - audit of products

» Stationary upholstery, non-leather
» Stationary upholstery, leather
» All coordinated chairs in upholstery vignettes listed

**AFTERNOON** Sales manager, self learning

» Sectionals, one-by-one
» Final hour for Q&A and review of products audited

## DAY FIVE

**MORNING** Sales manager

» Computer training, hands-on practice, case studies

**AFTERNOON** New hires — self study

» Recliner/motion category audit
» Final hour for Q&A and review of products audited

## DAY SIX

**MORNING** Sales manager, merchandise manager or assigned salesperson

» Category review case goods — one hour
» Category audit continues — self study

**AFTERNOON** Sales manager

» Customer engagement strategy to your selling system
» Define room planning, in-home processes

## DAY SEVEN

**MORNING** Sales manager, or assigned salesperson, or office person
- ◈ Computer training on office systems:
  - » Cash
  - » Credit card processing
  - » Financing processing

**AFTERNOON** New hires
- ◈ Product category audit continues — self study

## DAY EIGHT

**MORNING** Sales manager or assigned salesperson or office person
- ◈ Computer training
  - » Sales order entry
  - » Inventory lookup
  - » Special order processing

**AFTERNOON** Sales manager, merchandise manager or assigned salesperson
- ◈ Final product/category review
- ◈ Special order training

## DAY NINE

**MORNING** Sales manager
- ◈ The customer engagement strategy in greater detail — sketching, room planning
- ◈ In-home strategy for maximum customer satisfaction

**AFTERNOON**
- ◈ Customer engagement strategy
- ◈ Icovia Room Planner training

## DAY TEN

**MORNING** Sales manager — Vendor reps
- ◈ Product reviews

**AFTERNOON** Sales manager — Vendor reps
- ◈ Product reviews

## DAYS ELEVEN THROUGH THIRTEEN — Mentoring

» To be spent on the floor in shadow training with an experienced salesperson to learn what it's like at the point of contact, without being responsible for anything happening. Mentor will work with & assist salesperson in all aspects of the job.

## DAY FOURTEEN

» Customer engagement strategy

» Using Trax or other CRM system

## DAY FIFTEEN

» Open for review of all aspects of the training.

» Testing

» Critique from both sides

» Performance review with shadow trainer and sales manager

» Get set to go!

The above will be adjusted to your store's organization and structure and to the limitations of your staff, but we urge you to develop a written format and agenda for all new hire training to ensure that the job gets done completely and correctly.

## Appendix B
## Room Design Profile Form

| | |
|---|---|
| NAME: | PHONE: |
| ADDRESS: | CITY/ZIP: |
| SALESPERSON: | DATE: |
| E-MAIL: | BEST TIMES: |
| ROOM TYPE: | DIMENSIONS: |
| DESIRED LOOK: | PREFERED COLORS: |
| HOW USED? | FOCAL POINT: |
| PREF. FABRICS: | LIGHTING: |
| CHILDREN: | FLOORING: |
| SEATING FOR: | WALLS: |
| PETS OR OTHER NEEDS: | |

ROOM SKETCH (Include all architectural elements):

## FURNITURE SELECTIONS

| STYLE # | DESCRIPTION- COVER | MEASURE- MENTS | QTY | REG PRICE | SALE PRICE | PROMO DATE |
|---------|--------------------|----------------|-----|-----------|------------|------------|
|         |                    |                |     |           |            |            |
|         |                    |                |     |           |            |            |
|         |                    |                |     |           |            |            |
|         |                    |                |     |           |            |            |
|         |                    |                |     |           |            |            |
|         |                    |                |     |           |            |            |
|         |                    | DELIVERY       |     |           |            |            |
|         |                    | SUB-TOTAL      |     |           |            |            |
|         |                    | SALES TAX      |     |           |            |            |
|         |                    | TOTAL          |     |           |            |            |

## FOLLOW-UP ACTION PLAN

| NEXT ACTION | DATE/TIME | RESULT |
|-------------|-----------|--------|
|             |           |        |
|             |           |        |
|             |           |        |

ADDITIONAL NOTES:

## Appendix C
## Floor Product Audit Process

Floor product audits are performed by individuals or teams of new sales employees to completely familiarize them with all the furniture on your selling floor. Teams work together to learn together and to help create a bond among them so they don't feel isolated on the floor. This audit can take up to five days to complete, but it is very important.

Experienced people can help inexperienced people understand things they wouldn't otherwise be exposed to.

This works in conjunction with rep training, as they perform product training.

Here are the rules:

- ⟐ The process begins with a classroom overview of vendors by a manager (see attached).
- ⟐ New sales employee study and complete one major category at a time.
- ⟐ Employees fill out a form for each group or item on the floor. Each person fills out his or her own copy of this form, as the group examines and researches each group so they have a record of having touched, sat in, and discussed every group on the floor.
- ⟐ Employees study and complete each category one at a time before moving on to another group:
  - » Bedroom — Master — Adult
  - » Bedroom — Youth
  - » Stationary upholstery – including wicker and rattan
  - » Motion upholstery
  - » Recliners
  - » Casual dining
  - » Formal dining
  - » Home office

> » Wall units and entertainment furniture
> » Occasional tables and other accent furniture
> » Bedding (should be done with manufacturing representative)

Employees write down any questions and meet with their sales manager at the end of each day to review progress and ask questions.

## FLOOR PRODUCT AUDIT FORMS

| | |
|---|---|
| **CATEGORY:** | |
| **VENDOR:** **VSN:** | **ITEM/GROUP NAME:** |
| **DESCRIPTION**<br><br>**WOODS:** **FINISH:**<br><br>**FABRIC AND GRADE:**<br><br>**AVAILABLE IN LEATHER?** | |
| **GROUP/ITEM PRICE RANGE:** | |
| **ITEMS IN GROUP NOT SHOWN: (NOTE PRICE RANGE)** | |

CATEGORY:

VENDOR:      VSN:          ITEM/GROUP NAME:

DESCRIPTION


WOODS:                FINISH:

FABRIC AND GRADE:

AVAILABLE IN LEATHER?

GROUP/ITEM PRICE RANGE:

## Appendix D
## Room Design Information Workbook

| | |
|---|---|
| Name: | Date: |
| Address: | Home phone:<br><br>Work:<br><br>Cell:<br><br>E-mail: |

| | |
|---|---|
| Room Description: | Use: |
| Preferred look and feel: | Color scheme:<br><br><br>Floors/Walls: |
| Family information: | Samples required: |

| | |
|---|---|
| Home visit appointment day/date/time: | Appointment verified: |

Customer:

## INITIAL FURNITURE/FABRIC SELECTIONS IN STORE

| Style # | Cover/Color/ Description | Measure-ments | Qty. | Reg. Price | Sale Price | Promo End Date |
|---------|--------------------------|---------------|------|------------|------------|----------------|
|  |  |  |  |  |  |  |
|  |  |  |  |  |  |  |
|  |  |  |  |  |  |  |
|  |  |  |  |  |  |  |
|  |  |  |  |  |  |  |
|  |  |  |  |  |  |  |
|  |  |  |  |  |  |  |
|  |  |  |  |  |  |  |
|  |  |  |  |  |  |  |
|  |  |  |  |  |  |  |
|  |  | Delivery Charge |  |  |  |  |
|  |  | Sub-Total |  |  |  |  |
|  |  | Sales Tax |  |  |  |  |
|  |  | Total |  |  |  |  |

## FINAL FURNITURE/FABRIC SELECTIONS IN STORE

| Style # | Cover/Color/ Description | Measure-ments | Qty. | Reg. Price | Sale Price | Promo End Date |
|---------|--------------------------|---------------|------|------------|------------|----------------|
|         |                          |               |      |            |            |                |
|         |                          |               |      |            |            |                |
|         |                          |               |      |            |            |                |
|         |                          |               |      |            |            |                |
|         |                          |               |      |            |            |                |
|         |                          |               |      |            |            |                |
|         |                          |               |      |            |            |                |
|         |                          |               |      |            |            |                |
|         |                          | Delivery Charge |    |            |            |                |
|         |                          | Sub-Total     |      |            |            |                |
|         |                          | Sales Tax     |      |            |            |                |
|         |                          | Total         |      |            |            |                |

In store presentation appointment
day/date/time:

## ACCESSORY SELECTION

| Style # | Description | Measure-ments | Qty. | Reg. Price | Sale Price | Promo End Date |
|---------|-------------|---------------|------|------------|------------|----------------|
|         |             |               |      |            |            |                |
|         |             |               |      |            |            |                |
|         |             |               |      |            |            |                |
|         |             |               |      |            |            |                |
|         |             |               |      |            |            |                |
|         |             |               |      |            |            |                |
|         |             |               |      |            |            |                |
|         |             |               |      |            |            |                |
|         |             |               |      |            |            |                |
|         | Sub-Total   |               |      |            |            |                |
|         | Delivery Charge |           |      |            |            |                |
|         | Sub-Total   |               |      |            |            |                |
|         | Sales Tax   |               |      |            |            |                |
|         | Total for Accessories |     |      |            |            |                |

## ROOM SKETCH WITH DETAILED MEASUREMENTS

## HOUSE CALL PROJECT CHECK LIST

| Task | Completed | Notes | Sales Mgr. Initials |
|---|---|---|---|
| Room sketch (plan) in store | | | |
| Initial product selections with pricing | | | |
| House call info. form | | | |
| Home visit appt. made (7-day limit) | | | |
| House call completed | | | |
| Digital photos taken | | | |
| All samples obtained | | | |
| Final selections made In home with final prices | | | |
| Presentation appt. made at home visit (7-day limit) | | | |
| Design work completed — formal layout | | | |
| Practice presentation made | | | |
| Presentation follows format | | | |
| Sale closed — first presentation | | $ | |

# Endnotes

1. See www.accenture.com/articles/customercentricity 0509
2. *Western Reporter* magazine June 2009 "Understanding the Furniture Purchase Decision"
3. See Furniture Today, "The List," (Winter 2008) dated November 24, 2008.
4. See the report "Eight Emerging Retail Trends to Deliver High Performance" from Accenture, a worldwide retail consulting firm at www.accenture.com.
5. *Furniture Today*, HGTV research by OTX Corporation. January 24, 2008 This partnership between the NHFA and HGTV was never consummated because of insufficient funding from industry retailers.
6. Roy H Williams, "The Wizard of Ads" See www.mondaymorningmemo.com for a detailed explanation of these two shopping modes by the man who thought it all up
7. Kotter, John P. *Leading Change* (Boston: Harvard Business School Press, 1996). You can read portions of this important book online by searching for John P. Kotter.

# About the Author

Joe Capillo has been managing, coaching, mentoring, and teaching salespeople and sales managers in the retail home furnishings industry for over 35 years. Since 1993, Joe has consulted with dozens of retail furniture companies on issues of performance management. His purpose has been to focus industry attention on the overriding importance of understanding all relevant sales metrics to improve individual performance and bring salespeople to their goals. His message has always been that the performance of our entire industry lies in the hands of the thousands of retail salespeople who are, for the most part, our industry's touching point with consumers and should receive a far higher level of attention than is usually experienced.

Joe has been a contributing editor of *Furniture World* magazine for over a decade and has spoken at many industry events and seminars.

# Index